Introducing Prehistory

Other titles in this series:

Cassell's Introducing Archaeology Series

Introducing Prehistory

AVRAHAM RONEN

Cassell · London

CASSELL & COMPANY LTD
Cassell & Collier Macmillan Publishers Ltd
35 Red Lion Square, London WC1R 4SG
and at Sydney, Auckland, Toronto, Johannesburg
and an affiliate of Macmillan Publishing Company Inc., New York

Designed by Ofra Kamar

First published in Great Britain 1976

I.S.B.N. 0 304 29472 1

Printed by Peli Press, Ltd., Givataim.
PRINTED IN ISRAEL

F. 875

CONTENTS

INTRODUCTION

Human history is customarily divided into two parts: the first from the appearance of man up to the invention of writing, and the second from the appearance of written documents to the present. The latter, commonly called *history*, is the only portion of the human past which is studied academically and is more or less widely known. The term *prehistory* was introduced to designate the pre-literate period of humanity. According to our present knowledge, more than 20 million years may have elapsed since the first fossils on the human line of evolution appeared. *History,* in the sense of written documents, covers at most the last 5,000 years, yet an understanding of the human phenomenon is often sought only in this negligible fraction of total human history. The view that attempts at this understanding are futile is widely held — as expressed in "the only thing that we learn from history is that we learn nothing from history", or "there is no new thing under the sun" (Ecclesiastes, i,19).

As far as the basic psycho-social properties of man (rather than his technology) are concerned, then indeed nothing new *has* happened under the sun in the last 5,000 years. In order to trace the formation of man and the emergence of his special characteristics, we must turn to that vast span of time, prehistory.

I   THE PROBLEM

The human phenomenon we wish to understand is man's present status in the surrounding world. The uniqueness of this status is clear: here is a creature who governs the world absolutely and yet does not differ in any significant way from the inhabitants of the animal world with which he shares his domain. Indeed, man is inferior to many animals as regards strength, speed, or defence organs; yet he has made himself the strongest and the fastest creature of all. Whereas all other living organisms can exist only within well defined environments of the globe, man has veritably no environmental boundaries; he survives in desert and polar regions, under the sea, and on the moon.

At the same time, however, this super-creature is bound by the laws that govern all the living world. Just as the lowest form of animal must eat and drink, so must man; man multiplies and man must die, just as animals reproduce and die.

"Simultaneously worms and gods", therein lies the human paradox as Maslow put it.[1] It is this situation which perplexes modern man as it did past generations, as witnessed in all philosophy and all religions. We look into the past, then, in the hope of understanding how the human paradox occurred; we expect that past events can explain the present situation.

Consider: why should man be concerned with this question in the first place? Why are you and I intrigued by it? Looking into the past will not make our foods more plentiful, nor our aircraft faster. Yet there are few human beings or groups of humans which do not wish to know their origins. In fact, all comprehend this knowledge in one way or another, be it Biblical tradition or that of the Hopi Indian, whether taught in schools or in the initiation ceremonies of illiterate groups. Why?

The question has been asked repeatedly. The answers invariably add up to "human restlessness and anguish" which results in a "thirst for knowledge".[2] Implicit in these answers is the fact that universal human concern with the human situation is a *necessity*, not just curiosity. This necessity would seem to stem from the human phenomenon as a whole, since apparently no other animal attempts to seek an explanation for its existence. Clearly then, the question "Why are we troubled?" cannot be answered, "Because we are human," since precisely how and why we are human was our starting point. "Restlessness" and "thirst for knowledge" only describe, they do not explain.

At this point we ought to broaden the terms of the question. Why it is necessary for man to seek understanding in *general*, not only of his present or past — why is he troubled at all, what drives him to search?

I entirely agree with the opinion that at the base of human restlessness and anxiety lies the knowledge of death. Knowledge of death requires awareness of future and past — that is, of time. Man is indeed unique among all animals in understanding the concepts of death and time. Of course, there can be no study of the past without the realization of its existence in the first place.

More precisely, it is my opinion that human anxiety stems not merely from the knowledge of death, but from the *fear* of death, and of the unknown future in general. Man's real need is *not* only to understand his present para-doxical situation, and still less to know his past history. What he is really after is escape from the fear of the unknown and the ability to foretell his future. As Piveteau put it, "If man seeks to know where he comes from, it is in the hope of learning where he is going."[3] And this can only be done, so man believes, by broadening not only his knowledge of his past, but his entire knowledge, since all the elements are, or might be, inter-related and could bear upon man. Thus, the study of history is expected to reveal the laws that govern human behaviour so that man can foretell his future behaviour; since we live on earth, our fates seem related, so let us study the sciences of earth. Since the stars too may affect man's existence, astrology, and later astronomy, become a focus of interest. And so on without end. Science is egocentric, in the sense that it stemmed from man's concern about himself and from his self-awareness.

As well as being a "tool-maker" and a "cultural animal", man is also a "fortune-teller". Furthermore, as we shall see in the following pages, fortune-telling is the only characteristic entirely restricted to man; tool-making and culture are, to some extent, shared by other animals as well. Before we find out how all this occurred in pre-history, let us first consider how pre-history is studied.

II METHODS OF STUDYING PREHISTORY

The study of prehistory is based upon such remains as have survived from those remote days. Analysis and dating allow them to be placed in order in time and space; in addition, an interpretation of them is needed to place them in an intelligible sequence of events.

It is widely held that archaeologists try to understand ancient man through the remains he has left behind. But, since the remains themselves provide no explanation, we really seek to understand them from what we know of ourselves, of our society, of other societies, of "primitive" human groups, and of the animal way of life, especially that of apes and monkeys. The facts — the remains — of prehistory are there but their linking together into what seems to be a coherent story is formulated by us.

It is true then, that while we seek to understand the present through the past, at the same time, "The past can be understood only through the present."[4]

1. *Difficulties*

The difficulties encountered in the study of prehistory are numerous. First, only a small portion of remains is known to us after only a century and a half of searching. Furthermore, different parts of the earth are unequally documented; some regions have been better explored than others and more remains brought to light there. Secondly, no direct evidence has survived of such aspects of past culture as language, social organization, or beliefs. Conclusions can only be indirectly deduced from the remains. Thirdly, that part of the material culture made of perishable materials (wood, leather, and so on) is normally destroyed.

These difficulties, both objective (data) and subjective (interpretation), call for great caution. It is clear that the account of prehistory is incompletely known; it is open to several opinions, may be recounted in more than one way and will certainly be modified as research progresses.

2. *Remains and their Recovery*

Remains are found either embedded in sediments or exposed on the surface of the earth. In the latter case, it can be assumed that the remains were eroded at one time or another, which greatly reduces their scientific value. Surface finds are important mainly because they suggest that somewhere in their vicinity a still-buried site or sites may exist. The great majority of the world's undisturbed prehistoric sites — that is, those buried underground — were discovered in this way. Buried sites are found both in caves and out in the open. Although prehistoric man is commonly portrayed as a "cave dweller", he actually dwelt mostly in open spaces, except for certain periods during which caves seem to have been preferred, where they existed.

The remains in a prehistoric site are uncovered by excavation. Since the remains are of an extremely diverse nature, and since many of them may be fragile and require careful attention, modern excavation is a delicate and costly procedure. The study of the remains is carried out by many different specialists: each analyses his own part of the find, and then compares results with the others to reconstruct the overall picture as completely as possible.

The remains can be classified according as to whether they are directly or indirectly connected with man. Those directly connected are the remains of man himself and of his culture: human bones, which are studied by the physical anthropologist; and all man-made objects (such as tools and constructions — walls, depressions in the ground, wind-breaks, floors, art objects, etcetera), which are investigated by the archaeologist.

Indirectly connected with man are those remains which inform us of the prehistoric environment of the site in question. The type of deposit in which the site is buried (soil, sand, gravel, etcetera) is studied by the geologist and the pedologist. Animal bones (from food animals, rodents, and other microfauna) are studied by the palaeozoologist; plant remains, either seeds or pollen, are studied by the palaeobotanist and the palinologist respectively. Chemists and other specialists are occasionally called upon to solve specialized problems.

The recovery of all these remains is done both at site and in the laboratory, and the results obtained — undreamt of one generation ago — are due to the recently developed techniques and excavation methods now at our disposal.

It is a well known fact that, once excavated, a site ceases to exist: the same evidence cannot be recovered

A Late Palaeolithic open-air site partly exposed from its sand cover on the coast of Israel. Grid marked by sticks

more than once. The knowledge that he is constantly recovering evidence at the price of its destruction lays a heavy burden on the excavator. One sees what one is looking for; but there may always be something which no one was looking for during the original excavation but which may turn out to be important later, when the site no longer exists. These considerations make prehistoric excavations the most meticulous (and slow) in the field of archae-

Entrance to the cave of Sefunim, Israel, with collapsed ceiling in front

ology. Pre-historians record in their field-notes a far broader range of observations than do excavators of historic sites. Samples are kept from every deposit which is eventually discarded. The sections of the layers are drawn in as much detail as possible. The position of all items found is carefully noted, because a certain pattern may exist that could pass unnoticed during the actual excavation. All the excavated deposits are sifted and/or floated in water for the recovery of grains, seeds, microfauna and other tiny remains which easily escape the eyes of the excavator. Even with all these precautions we are certain to miss hidden information. Some day, these data will be extracted in future excavations by methods still more advanced than those we use at present.

Here is an example of how the significance attached to certain prehistoric remains has changed within the last generation. At one time, an archaeologist would have done well had he correctly distinguished the layers in a site and then carefully reported their content of, say, tools and fireplaces. The most significant tools would have been kept and the rest would have been thrown away. The fireplaces would have yielded no information and naturally none of their contents would have been kept. Thus, the only knowledge acquired was what types of culture succeeded each other, and whether all used fireplaces or not.

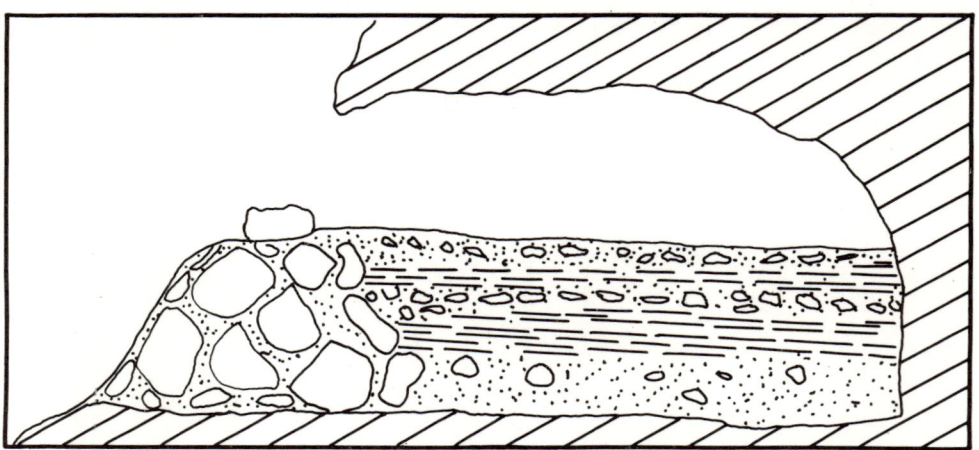

Archaeological layers schematically rendered in a vertical section done in 1925 (Saliha cave, Israel. Excavation Thurville-Petre)

Today, the careful mapping of tools and fireplaces shows us the plan of the dwelling at each occupational layer. In this way, the "kitchen" area, sleeping quarters, area of tool manufacture, entrances and pathways can be located.

Fireplaces are analysed for their fuel content (wood, fat, feces). Under laboratory tests, burned stones or bones may disclose the temperature of a particular fire. Thus it becomes possible to distinguish between high-temperature cooking fires and smaller fires used for warmth or light. Burned organic material is used for dating, as we shall see later on.

The nature and amount of information gathered in these two types of excavations (one carried out some time ago and the other as practised today) differ so radically that it is hard to believe only thirty years or so have elapsed between them. When we compare the contents of the different layers of the modern excavation, we have more than the form of tools alone to

Vertical section of archaeological layers drawn in a modern excavation. Dots represent artifacts (Caminade, France. Excavation D. de Sonneville-Bordes)

distinguish between various cultures. We have also the settlement pattern and a glimpse of some of the daily habits for each period of occupation. We gain a closer view of extinct groups of people; and the more we know about them, the closer we come to understanding them.

In that example I mentioned only tools and fireplaces. But, in modern excavations, all types of remains are analysed in greater detail than they were. Animal bones are now studied not only for the determination of their species but also for the way in which the bones were cut or split, the number of animals at the site and hence the quantity of meat they represent. The analysis of sediment and its content of animal, plant and snail species serves to give an indication of the environment within which the site existed. Students are aware of the fact that climatic changes occurred in the past and, once reconstructed, these enable us to perceive cultural change within its ecological milieu. We thereby gain an insight into how man adapted to his environment and how, simultaneously, he acted upon the environment.

The techniques involved in the recovery and analysis of each class of remains are complicated, and their details are too numerous to elaborate upon. Dealing with such a diversity of remains and working with so many

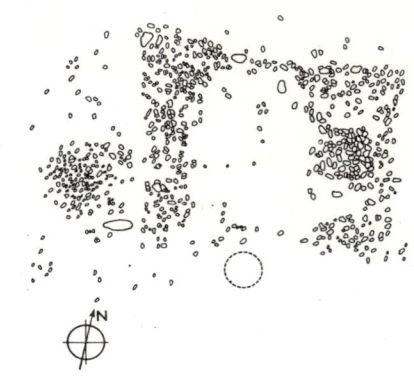

The position of every stone and artifact carefully noted on a horizontal plan (Mussidan, France. Excavated Gaussin and Bordes)

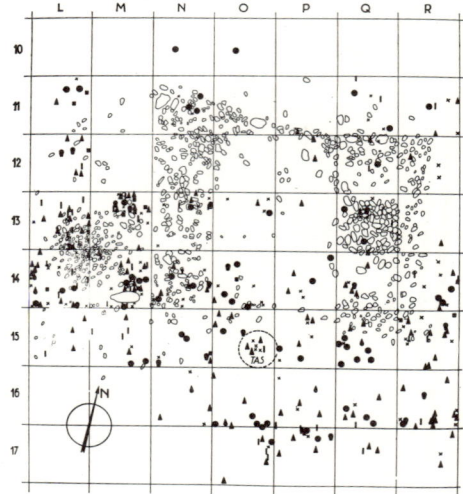

Location of stones alone hints at an organized pattern at Mussidan

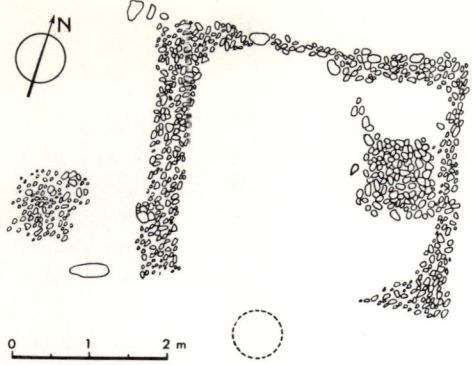

The reconstructed plan of a rectangular hut at Mussidan, some 15,000 years old

specialists makes the task of the prehistoric archaeologist more and more difficult. The co-ordination of all this information plus the comparison of final results with a vast and ever-growing body of data from other sites is rapidly forcing this area of study into the age of computers.

3. Methods of Dating

The most commonly used method of dating is the stratigraphic principle, which holds that in any normal succession of layers, or strata, the bottom one is the oldest and the top the most recent. Using this principle, one can correctly state that the human culture embedded in Layer A is younger than the culture in the underlying Layer B. Thus, we date A in relation to B, or B in relation to A; hence this method allows for *relative* dating. Still unanswered is the question: how old are both cultures.

Several methods are used for *absolute* dating, the most important of which is radioactive measurement. This method was devised only in 1948, and is still being improved. It is carried out in specialized laboratories on samples submitted by the excavator, and the procedure is based on the fact that some natural elements decay or change into other elements *at a constant rate*. Once this rate is established, dating is possible, as the following example will illustrate. All living organisms contain carbon including, in a fixed ratio, carbon 14 (C14), a radioactive element. When the organism dies, C14 starts to decay. Its ratio to the normal carbon changes, so that after 5570 years, only half of the original content of C14 remains. After the same timespan passes once more — that is, 11,140 years after death occurred — the ratio is reduced by another one-half, so that it is now a quarter of the original content, and so forth. The period 5570 years is called the 'half-life' of C14. After about nine such periods, or about 50,000 years, the amount left in the dead organism is so low that it is no longer detectable by present measuring devices. Today, carbon 14 provides the major basis of our time-table during the last 50,000 years.

Dates obtained by C14 measurements are expressed as, for example, 10,300 ± 170 B.P., meaning 10,300 years (give or take 170 years, the measurement's margin of error) before the present; that is, by international agreement, before AD 1950. The same date can be given as 9350 BC.

Other radiocarbon elements are used to date occurrences older than 50,000 years of age. The most widely used is potassium (K40), which decays at a fixed rate to form the gas argon (A40). With this method millions of years can be measured and thus the entire history of human life lies within measurable range.

III   THE CREATURE MAN

According to the Bible, mankind began as part of the divine creation. Man's special role in nature was clearly defined in the command: "And God blessed them, and God said unto them, Be fruitful and multiply and replenish the earth, and subdue it: and have domination . . . over every living thing that moveth upon the earth" (Genesis, i,28). This sets forth the same basic problem posed in the beginning of our book, namely, the human paradox. The divine command was taken as a satisfactory explanation until the emergence of modern science, or, more precisely, of two revolutionary developments: the first being the Darwinian theory of evolution, and the second the discovery of ancient fossils which looked human but were clearly of a more primitive type than modern man. These human fossils — Neanderthal man (discovered 1856) and Java man (discovered 1892) — strengthened the theory that man is subject to the process of evolution. That humanization is a matter of a gradual evolution from an animal level became the most perplexing notion brought forth by modern science.

In order to locate the point of divergence between human being and animal, we first must define what separates man from animal. Although we should be concerned primarily with those human traits visible in the archaeological record, these traits cannot be separated from the entire human phenomenon as it is understood today.

1.   *Bipedalism and Tool-Making*

What *does* separate human from animal? Apparently everything. Anatomically, man's erect posture and bipedalism (locomotion on two legs) are unique; as is his lack of any specialized defence organ, such as long teeth or claws.

All the other specifically human traits that come to mind belong to the realm of culture. Awareness of time and death has already been mentioned; one can add speech, education, technology and the possession of rituals and

Baboon in a threatening position

institutions. In effect, it is hard to find any one element that has not been "culturized" by man, even the most elementary needs like feeding or breeding. "Culture" is not easy to define because of its extremely diverse aspects; in its most general sense, it is "the total extrasomatic (non-anatomical) things man has or knows".[5] All the human traits, anatomical and cultural, are interrelated, influencing and being influenced by one another.

That erect posture is a precondition for humanization was already clear to the Greek philospher Anaxagoras in the 5th century BC. He wrote that "Man is intelligent because he has hands", meaning he is intelligent because his hands are freed from the task of locomotion. This enables him to compensate for the lack of fighting organs by making or using tools — whether these are crude sticks or bronze daggers is of secondary importance. At the same time, it can be argued that the degeneration of fighting organs is the result of using tools. Here, one cannot clearly distinguish cause from effect. The lack of anatomical specialization enabled man to become the highly adaptive creature he is, because tools, clothes and dwellings can be modified to fit different environments, whereas claws, teeth and fur can not.

The act of tool-making, even of the simplest ones, has more to it than might appear at first glance. Apart from good co-ordination of eyes, hands and fingers, it requires foresight and a planning capacity that enables man to envisage the object before its manufacture is begun; what James Deetz called "a mental template".[6] Tool-making has to do with the brain, as well as with the hands; both improved mutually. Hands capable of a more delicate performance (inferred from the archaeological record by the degree of perfection of tools) denote a more human or more intelligent brain. In the human brain, the centres controlling the hands are far more evolved than those commanding the feet, whereas in monkeys these centres are equally developed.

Thus, erect posture, free hands and intelligence lie at the root of man's most extraordinary achievement — culture. The many complicated elements which make up culture must be communicated and learned, and this is not possible without language and suitable conditions for learning — be it how to use a spear or a table fork. Like man's culture, his language and learning conditions are unique. Let us see why.

2.   *Language and Learning*

The anatomical organs with which we speak are identical to those of the ape. A parrot can even imitate every human sound. Yet neither apes nor parrots have devised a language in the human sense of the word. The main difference between human and animal language is man's capacity for objectification, again a matter of the brain and not of the speech organs. Objectification means giving objects specific names. It requires, in the first place, the clear distinguishing of objects from their surroundings, for instance, a tree from a forest. (The anatomical prerequisite for this is stereoscopic vision, shared by all monkeys and apes as well as man.)

In the second place, objectification calls for a capacity for abstraction, or symbolization, since there is really nothing in common between a wooden object topped with leaves and the word *tree.* There are words which symbolize more complicated objects, requiring a still higher degree of abstraction: thus *red* stands for flowers as well as for blood while *hope* stands for nothing that can be seen or touched. As far as we know, animals do not objectify.

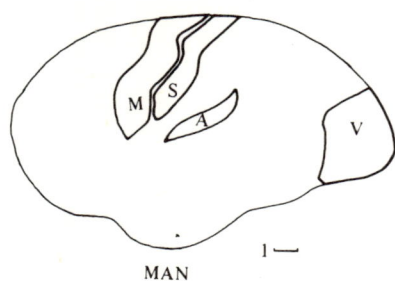

MAN

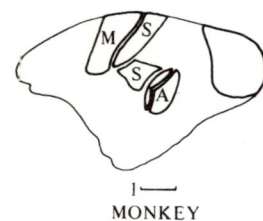

MONKEY

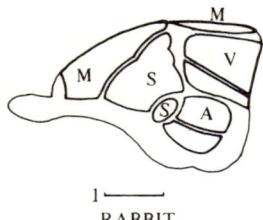

RABBIT

Since all human beings cry in the same way, but do not speak the same language, it is clear that language is learned, as is tool-making and one's entire culture. Indeed, another definition of culture says that it is "the total set of learned behaviour that one needs to live successfully".[7]

The more there is to be learned, the longer the time and the higher the intelligence required. Human beings require a far greater body of knowledge to survive than any animal and, in effect, the major difference between the human brain and that of an ape is that the frontal part of man's brain is larger; it is here that the areas responsible for learning speech and memory are located. At the same time, in the human brain there is a relative reduction of the portion involved in the sensory and motion functions.

The most favourable conditions for learning exist during infancy and youth, or from birth until full maturity is reached. Man's period of postnatal growth is longer than of other animals: it takes the first twenty years of life for

Motor and sensory systems in the brains of rabbit, monkey and man. In man, these systems involve the smallest portion of the cortex (A — auditory. M — motor. S — somatic. V — visual)

man to acquire physical and intellectual maturity, as against eleven years in the great apes and seven years in monkeys. In addition, chimpanzee and man are both born with a brain of about 350 cc; but a chimpanzee has only one-quarter of its total brain volume to grow until maturity (450 cc), whereas man's brain has three-quarters of its volume to develop (approximately to 1500 cc). This implies that a newborn chimpanzee is relatively more mature than man is at birth, which is indeed the case. While a chimpanzee infant can cling to its mother almost immediately after birth, and can search for food several weeks later, the human infant remains completely helpless for a much longer period. But man's immaturity at birth and long infancy period are extremely favourable for the teaching, or conditioning, of his behaviour, and hence for transmitting culture.

Extreme dependence and a long period of child care have a profound effect on the mother—infant relationship. It seems that the tighter the mother—child bond, the more affection there is between the two. Thus with baboons, where child-rearing is done by the entire group and not especially by the mother, mother—child relations lack affection and last for a shorter period than among gorillas, where the mother takes care of her offspring almost exclusively. We may infer from this that the mother—child bond in the case of early man was already stronger than among apes.

In the model of hominization presented here we wished to stress that the characteristic human traits are interrelated; a matter of process involving mutual development. Although the anatomical traits and a part of the cultural complex alone are clearly seen in the archaeological record, this model permits certain indirect inferences on some non-visible traits as well.

3. Man's Ancestors

Having summarized the principal characteristics of the human branch, let us turn to the animal level from which man could have diverged. For a long time it was believed that this divergence was a matter of culture versus an entire lack of culture. However, observation of animals in their natural habitat (rather than in captivity), mainly carried out since the 1960s, surprisingly indicated that actually the divergence took place from one certain level of culture to another; in other words, that there is a certain "animal culture".[8]

It became apparent from these studies that some social and behavioural patterns in monkeys and apes are learned, rather than being innate or instinctive. These include, for example, established ways of begging for food and of greeting a fellow chimpanzee, whether by chest-beating or touching hands (!) or hips. Noisy festivities were recorded among chimpanzees; these perhaps took place when two groups met each other. Tool-making in its true sense was also observed: this involved the creation of a short, thin stick used to pierce a termite-hill, so that the termites which cling to the stick could be eaten. To make this tool a shoot is broken off to the desired length. Rudimentary as it may seem, it is nevertheless tool-*making* with a "model" borne in mind, not just tool-*using* which was commonly considered to be an animal's only capability. There is even more to this, since the chimpanzee has been observed to prepare a termite-stick when no termite hills were in sight — that is, without an immediate stimulus. This points to a planning capacity, or foresight equal to that of a man preparing a trap before game is sighted. That a mental capacity is involved is clearly shown by the fact that although baboons watch chimpanzees probing for termites, and although baboons too are fond of the insects, a baboon was never seen trying to imitate the technique.

While mainly vegetarian, apes are known to consume meat occasionally. They show a degree of co-operation in the hunt of animals such as rabbits or monkeys, and then share the kill.[9] Co-operation and sharing are also typically human behaviour, part of the learned culture.

A human cultural trait of broad concern is the universal presence of an incest taboo, meaning, "that in human society a man must obtain a woman from another man who gives him a daughter or a sister" as put by Levi-Strauss.[10] Long observations of Macaque monkeys in Japan (continuously since 1953) show an effective prohibition against incest prevailing in the troop: not a single time in thousands did copulation involve a mother and her son.[11] So this, too, ceases to be exclusively a human trait.

Observations of the animal way of life began only a very short time ago. As yet we know little about animal culture in general, and about that particular level from which man initially came. Today, however, the difference between human and animal is an absolute one, as much as that between spacecraft and termite-probes. But only subtle differences are expected to have existed at the point of divergence. The differences were subsequently to become clearer and more accentuated as each branch proceeded on its own course. Probably a simple matter of quantity at the beginning, gradually the gap between man and animal widened until, at some point, the difference became a matter of quality rather than of quantity. The extremes of this process — the primates on one hand and modern man, civilized or 'primitive', on the other — are better known than the various phases along the way. The process took millions of years, and surely went through many more stages than those we are presently able to distinguish in the archaeological record.

In our view, the main phases in the process of humanization are (1) the initial human phase, (2) the intermediate phase and (3) the attainment of full humanity, all of which we shall now proceed to describe.

IV   THE INITIAL HUMAN PHASE

For the sake of perspective, let us remember that the earth has existed for some five billion years and life for three billion. The first vertebrates appeared 500 million years ago and the first mammals 200 million years ago. The oldest fossil thought to be on the human line of evolution is about 25 million years of age. It is called *Ramapithecus* (*Rama* is an Indian god, *Pithecus* means ape in Greek). This fossil was discovered in India, but similar remains were later found in Europe and Africa as well.

This fossil is considered para-human by virtue of its anatomical traits, in particular its small canine teeth. Large canines are a primate's most effective weapon and tool, whereas small canines are characteristic of man. The degeneration of canines in *Ramapithecus* must have been compensated for by other means. Indeed, the degeneration may have been an outcome of a growing dependency on tools. Thus, anthropologists maintain that because *Ramapithecus* could not feed and fight

the way other primates did, perhaps he had to do so more the way a human does. This implies tool-making, for which quite an intensive use of the hands would be needed, which in turn requires an advanced form of uprightness. Furthermore, as we have already noted, the greater the dependency on tool-making the more must be learned, hence the possibility of a long period of child dependency has been argued for *Ramapithecus.* [12]

The fact that *Ramapithecus* had such a wide geographical range of habitation, stretching from western Europe to India, suggests a good adaptive capacity for varying environments — another trait that has its ultimate expression in modern man.

It is generally believed that the new mode of behaviour involving bipedalism and intensive tool-making was initiated as an adaptive response to a change of environment, namely a shift from life in the forest to life in the open grass-land (a shift perhaps caused by a reduction of world forest space under a gradual desiccation of the climate). This idea finds some support in the fact that chimpanzees who live in the dense African rain forest use bipedalism much less than chimpanzees who live in a more open type of forest.

The initial hint of an infra-human type of behaviour represented by *Ramapithecus* and similar remains is outside the scope of prehistoric archaeology, simply because archaeologists are as yet unable to recognize cultural remains from this primitive phase. Perhaps the tools used were wholly or largely unmodified rocks, perhaps they were made mainly of organic materials. In any case, skeletal remains are the only recognizable feature of this stage. The archaeologist's turn comes later when stone tools have become sufficiently modified to be properly distinguished from natural stones. At present, this occurrence is known to have taken place roughly three million years ago. For a long time it was held that man the tool-maker has existed for only one million years. It was only a decade or so ago that researchers overcame their reluctance as well as their surprise and accepted the radioactive date of about two million years ago as it applies to unquestionable human industry found in Olduvai Gorge in Tanzania, East Africa, by Louis and Mary Leakey. This date at once doubled the then known timespan of

human tool-making. The acceptance of the newest date for earliest tool-making — about three million years ago — was much easier; this was established from the findings at a site near Lake Rudolf in Kenya by Richard Leakey and his team in 1971.[13] Actually, a layer of lava covering the tools was dated to 2.6 million years ago. There is no apparent reason why this date will not further recede (perhaps even before this book is printed), and one can but wonder what point in time prehistory may reach.

What archaeologists call "their" initial human phase began then roughly three million years ago, when tool manufacture had already reached a level well beyond that of "animal culture". This human industry is termed "Oldowan" after Olduvai Gorge where it was uncovered for the first time. During this initial Oldowan phase, which until now has been found only in Africa, two types of bipedal creatures lived side by side in the Savannah, or open grassland: a member of the species *Homo*, that is, true man; and a close relative called *Australopithecus* (meaning ape of the southern hemisphere). The presence of true man so long ago is another surprising discovery made during the recent excavations near Lake Rudolf already mentioned. Prior to that discovery, the sole maker of Oldowan culture seemed to have been *Australo-*

pithecus and it was assumed that when true man first appeared, he was already equipped with more advanced tools. This assumption substantiated the general notion which held that major cultural advances were each related to a new and more advanced type of man. Recent research indicates, however, that this notion is wrong and that cultural evolution is not necessarily associated with physical evolution.[14]

1. *Material Culture*

Before describing the earliest known tools, we shall discuss the basic ideas of working stone. Basically, there is only one method, and that is to break off pieces of a stone by striking it with a hammer. This same method has been in use from the very start of stone tool manufacture to modern masons or sculptors, the only difference being the technical means by which the job is done. Archaeologists term the act of breaking-off "knapping" or "flaking", while the pieces removed are called "flakes". Flakes can be further worked by hammer blows, and this action is termed "trimming" or "retouching". The latter is done in a delicate manner and removes small fragments, generally

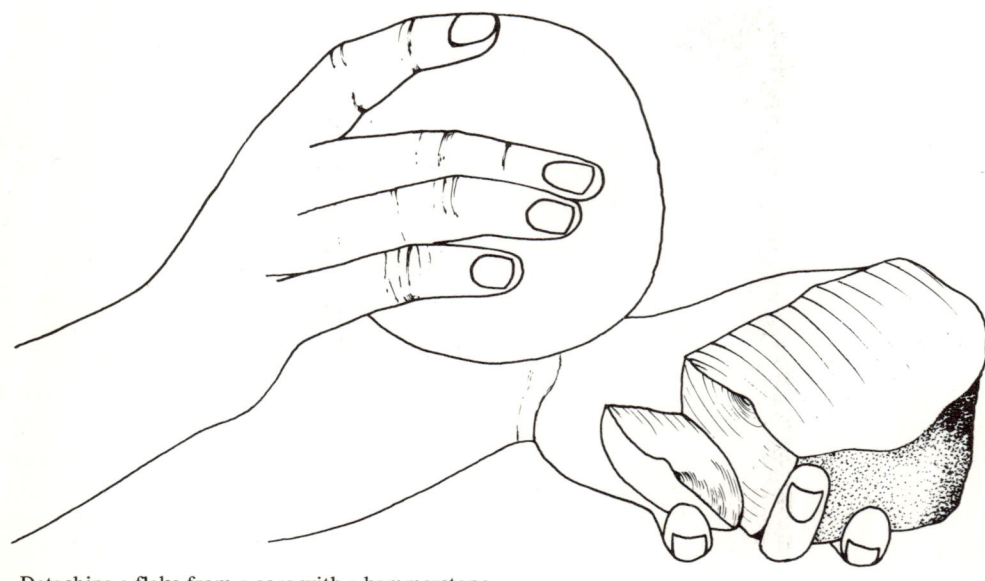

Detaching a flake from a core with a hammerstone

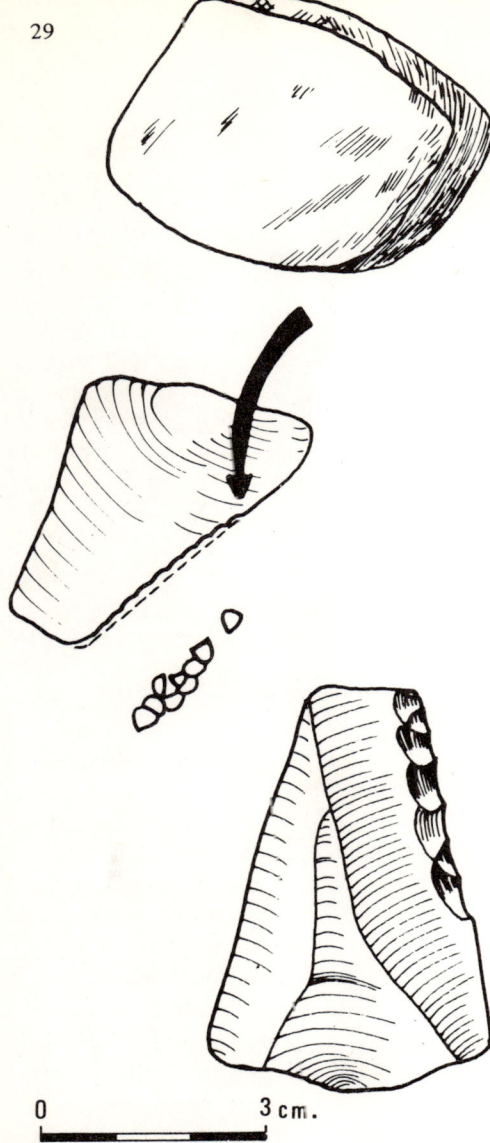

less than one centimetre in size, while the action of flaking produces larger pieces. Deliberate flaking can be distinguished from natural stone debris because a man-made flake is the result of a more or less violent blow at one edge of the flake (which is termed its base). The sudden shock caused by the blow travels along the stone in the form of concentric waves. Once the flake is detached it has a cone-shaped protuberance near the point of impact, and frequently also concentric ripples along its surface of detachment. Since the most natural common agents that split stones are slow processes (a chemical solution affecting fissures or temperature changes causing mechanical stress), the above characteristics of a sudden shock are rarely produced naturally. In the cases where stones may be subjected to nature's sudden blows, mainly on sea shores and in river beds, caution is required on the part of the archaeologist.

The commonest hammer used in pre-history is a stone of a suitable shape, size and weight, termed a "hammerstone". Stone-on-stone technique, regardless of whether a hammerstone or a stone-anvil is involved, is called "hard hammer", as opposed to the "soft hammer" method, introduced at a later period.

The Oldowan culture is characterized by the chopping tool*: a stone pebble, one edge of which was sharpened to

0   3 cm.

Retouching by striking lower face of flake removes tiny pieces and produces scars on opposite face.

*See appendix for stone tool nomenclature.

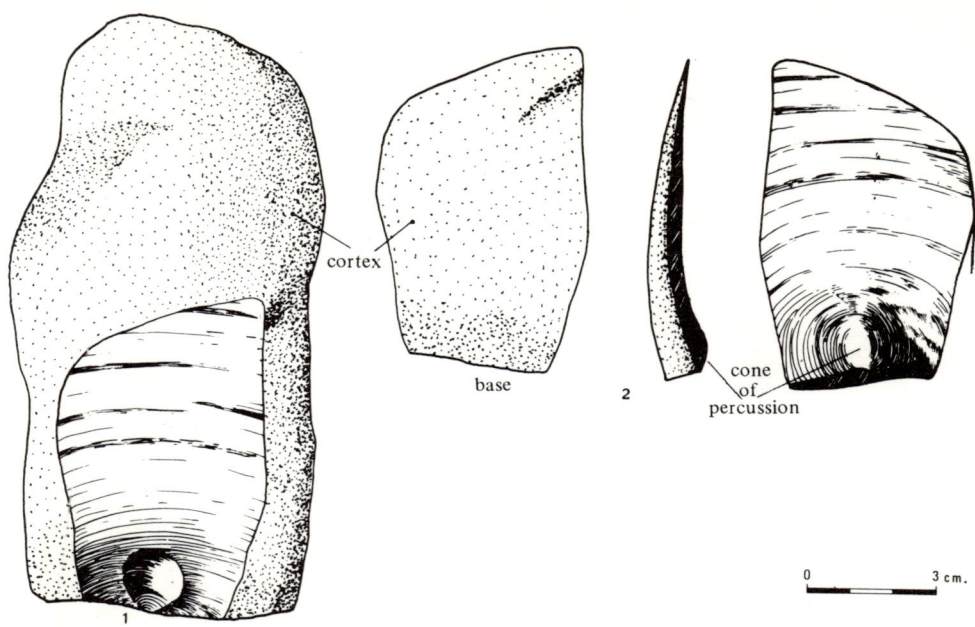

cortex

base

2

cone of percussion

0   3 cm.

1) Core with natural cortex and a flake-scar. 2) Both faces of the flake removed

form a cutting or chopping edge. This was done by the removal of a few flakes, and apparently hard hammer was the only method used. Some of the flakes obtained were also used as tools: a few show a deliberate retouch which shaped them into conventional tool forms such as scrapers* or notches*. Other flakes were put to use without being retouched, as can be seen from the utilization marks they bear: that is, irregular and discontinuous trimming on an otherwise sharp edge. The exact function of each tool is of course unknown; we can only guess by considering the everyday needs of early man,

and relying on our reasoning and ethnographical examples.

Oldowan-culture man must have required tools to skin animals and to cut their flesh, to cut and shape wood, to dig for roots or burrow for small animals; he needed weapons for both offensive and defensive purposes. These activities involved instruments for cutting, scraping, digging and piercing. Wood most likely played an important role in his tools, but none have survived. (Pointed sticks could have been used for digging, fighting and hunting.) We assume that sharp stone flakes served as knives for cutting soft matter,

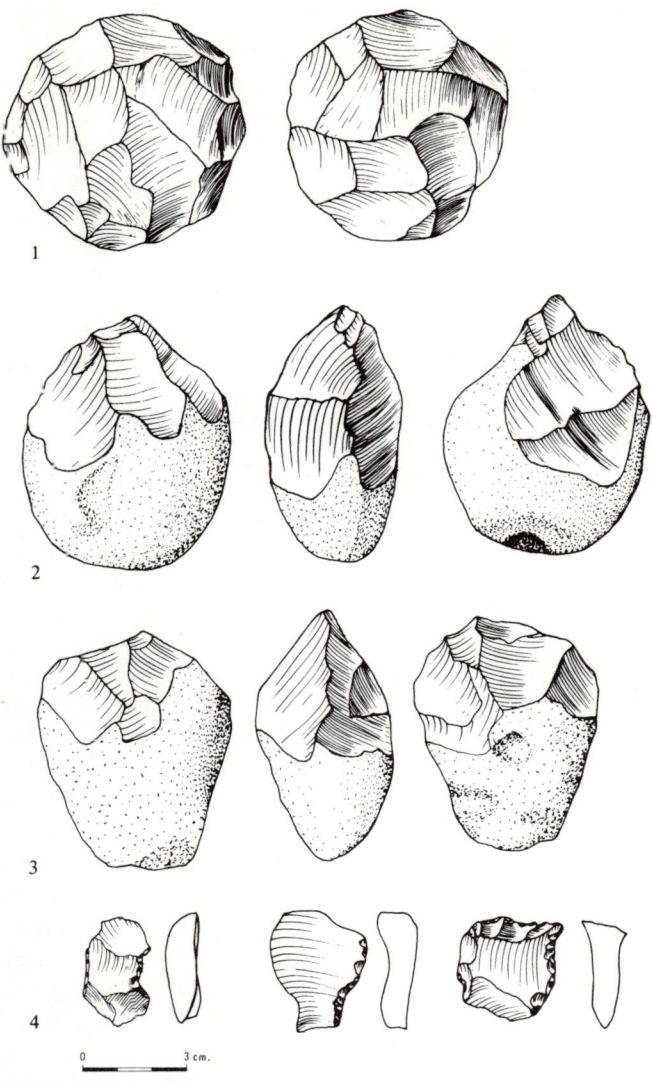

Oldowan tools. 1) Spheroid. 2, 3) Chopping-tools. 4) Flake tools

whereas chopping tools could have been useful for cutting branches or hard ligaments, smashing bone and other rough work. Choppers were probably multiple-purpose tools, and on the whole, a rather poor degree of tool specialization is believed to have existed in the Oldawan culture.

In the later and more evolved stage of the Oldowan culture, called "developed Oldowan", spheroids* are added to the tool kit. These were stones flaked all around into a spherical shape. The Oldowan culture ends when a new type of tool — the handaxe* — makes its appearance. Constituting at first a small, almost negligible addition to the total tool kit, handaxes progressively outnumber the chopping tools and become the characteristic element of the next major cultural phase, the Acheulean (so called after St Acheul in northern France).

2. Subsistence and Behaviour

The remains of animal bones at sites of the Oldowan cultural stage indicate a partly carnivorous diet — vegetation probably composed most of the diet, although remains are practically unknown. Animals of all sizes were eaten, but at present it seems that smaller animals such as young antelopes and pigs formed the major part of the meat menu. Remains of large animals such as the elephant, giraffe, buffalo or hippopotamus seem to be less numerous at the sites of this period, and it is impossible to determine if those present were hunted or found dead. Remains of frogs, reptiles and rodents were also found in refuse heaps and could have been consumed as well. This range of game exploitation seems wider than that practised by chimpanzees. *Australopithecus* may also have been hunted by the man of the Lake Rudolf type.

The behaviour which best characterizes the Oldowan culture, and distinguishes it from that of the ape, is a home-base type of dwelling. This is manifested by a localized cluster of all sorts of occupational refuse: tools, stone and bone debris, and sometimes a hint of construction. A home-base indicates that food was conveyed to the site for consumption, and hence that certain individuals stayed there for whom food had to be brought in by others. This behaviour is unlike that of apes, who consume food where it is found and do not leave collected refuse in any particular location. The home-base behaviour of early man reminds us of modern hunter-gatherers, where the old and the very young stay at home while adults forage for food. Normally, the women would seek vegetable food while the men would take care of animal hunting. Whether such a division of labour among the sexes existed in the

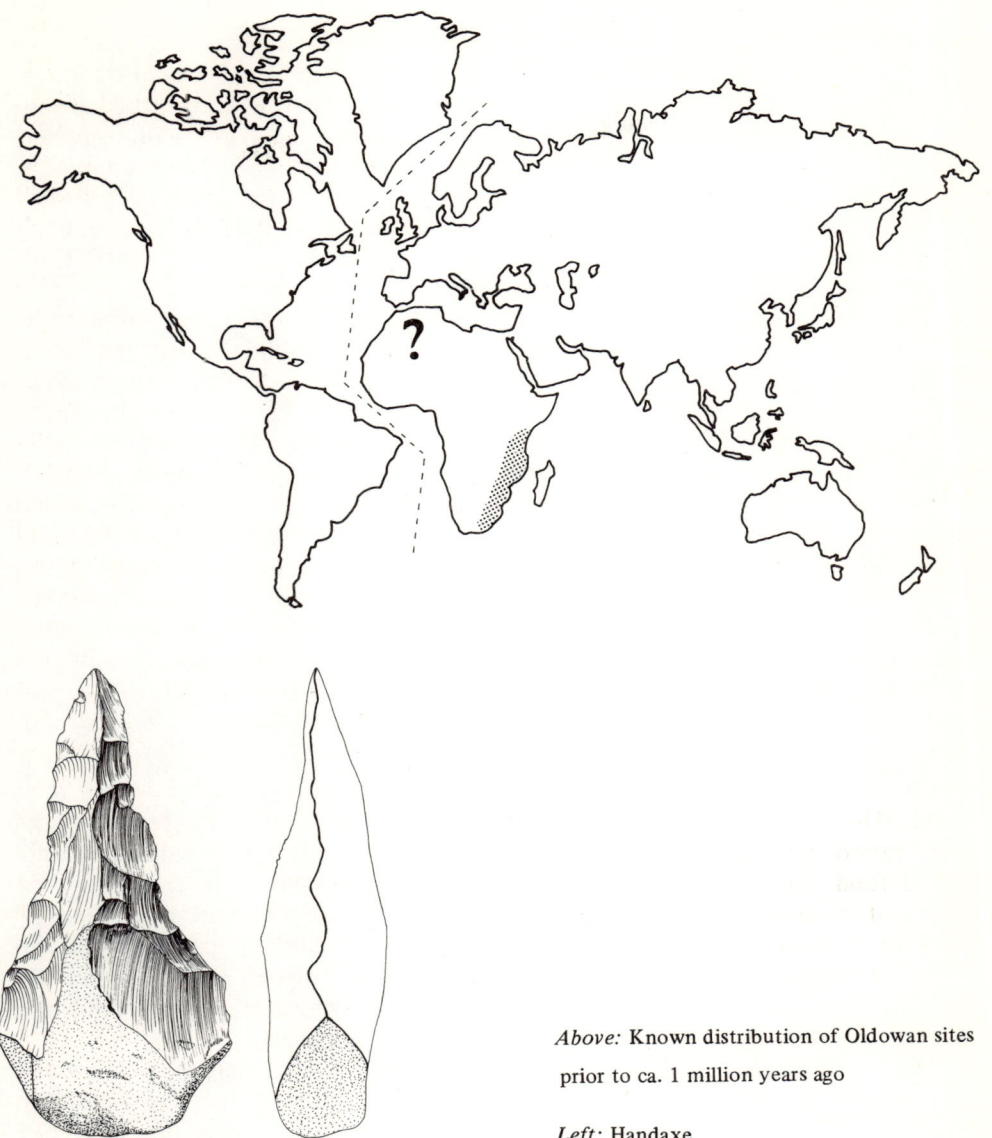

Above: Known distribution of Oldowan sites prior to ca. 1 million years ago

Left: Handaxe

Oldowan cultural stage cannot be directly inferred from archaeological finds. However, bearing in mind that even among chimpanzees hunting is mainly a male's job, it can be assumed that Olduvai man behaved in a similar fashion.

The existence of a home-base may perhaps suggest that child care was also different from what it is among apes, in that stronger ties already existed between adults (or parents?) and children. More prolonged and more intense child care goes together with a growing necessity to learn vitally important matters such as tool-making, tool employment, properties of various materials and so forth. Their teaching would require communication with at least some degree of human language, where objects and object-manipulation could be distinguished. Also, a home-base is a prerequisite for the human manner of treating old or sick persons, who get no assistance in the non-human world. The maintenance of a home-base, varied subsistence activities and regular food sharing may all point to a degree of communication that lies beyond the needs of non-human primates.

The home-bases known from the initial human phase range in area from 30 square metres to 300 square metres and more. The larger sites may represent several occupations of the same locality, but the smaller home-bases are similar in area to those occupied by a band or a family of modern hunter-gatherers. The few undisturbed living-floors known from this remote period are sharply delineated, which would suggest that some kind of physical border had existed, either a natural one such as bushes or an artificial wind-break of branches.

There are two important differences between the home-base of the initial human phase and the chimpanzee dwelling. First, the nest of leaves built in a tree by the chimpanzee serves one individual only, or at the most a mother and her offspring, whereas even the smallest human home-base must have served a larger number of individuals. Second, a chimpanzee normally builds a new nest every night, and it serves only for sleeping purposes. The human home-base clearly served other purposes besides sleeping — feeding and tool-making are quite evident — and it was most likely used for longer than one day, although it is extremely difficult to evaluate for exactly how long. Nevertheless, the home-base does not necessarily imply that a family-type organization already existed in the initial human phase; that is, a lasting bond between male, female or females and their offspring.

At present, the main body of known Oldowan culture is from Africa. Toward its end, during the developed

Oldowan stage, human population appears outside the African continent in the Near East, the Far East and Europe. Man now dwelt upon three continents and occupied an area that largely exceeded the ecological niche which apes occupy.

3. Degree of Humanization

The initial human phase in the archaeological sense of this term, that is the last three million years, is characterized by the existence of anatomically true man, associated with the Oldowan culture. His cranium capacity is estimated at 800 cc or more, as compared with 450 cc of the chimpanzee and 500 to 600 cc of *Australopithecus.* The numerous skeletal remains of the latter may now be interpreted as man's food refuse. It should be noted, however, that *Australopithecus* must also have depended upon tools for his survival since, like man, he too had small canines, walked upright, and lived in the large open grassland which is the carnivores' domain. Perhaps one day, a "man type" industry can be distinguished from an "*Australopithecus* type" within the overall Oldowan culture. *Australopithecus* seems to have disappeared close to the time of the

transition from the initial to the intermediate phase.

During the initial human phase, man was essentially a small-game hunter who dwelt in home-bases preferably near lakes or along stream beds. His tools were simple and showed a low degree of standardization, but nevertheless must have compensated successfully for the reduction of canines. Man's communication potential may be assumed to have been low, although it was perhaps more advanced than nonhuman language. The use of fire was apparently unknown during this stage.

To sum up, 'man' of the initial human phase, as reflected in the archaeological record, is clearly distinguished from other animals, both anatomically and by some distinct patterns of behaviour. And yet this being still seems an equal in nature, in the sense that he could have constituted prey as well as predator. This will no longer be the case in the next phase of human evolution, when man will opt out of the harmony of nature to which all other animals are subjected. The fundamental rupture between man and his surroundings occurs when man becomes the possessor of a power with which no other being is endowed — that is, fire.

V   THE INTERMEDIATE PHASE

We call "intermediate" the phase during which the differentiation between man and animal became absolute, but in which the archaeological record does not yet attest to full humanity from a psychological point of view. The intermediate phase lasted about one million years, and ended roughly 100,000 years ago.

There are several phenomena whose appearance mark the beginning of this phase; these are:

(1) The substitution of Oldowan culture by the Acheulean culture, characterized by the tool called a handaxe.

(2) The appearance of *Homo erectus,* with a cranial capacity of about 1000-1200 cc.

(3) The growing potential for big-game hunting, as opposed to primarily small-game hunting of the preceeding phase.

(4) The use of fire by man, which to us characterizes the intermediate phase. We do not know the exact order of appearance of these phenomena nor do we know the degree to which they may be inter-related. We shall examine them as various aspects of an overall new constellation.

1.   *Material Culture*

The transition from the chopping-tool of the Oldowan culture to the handaxe of the Acheulean required a better flaking ability: compared to a chopping tool, the handaxe required more numerous flake removals and a better control of hand movements, that is, a better coordination between eyes and hands which results in a better aim.

Right: Flint blade cores and blades

Overleaf left: "Venus" of Brassempuy, France, with either hair or hat depicted. Ca. 25,000 years old

Overleaf right: "Venus" of Laussel, France, holding a horn. Ca. 25,000 years old

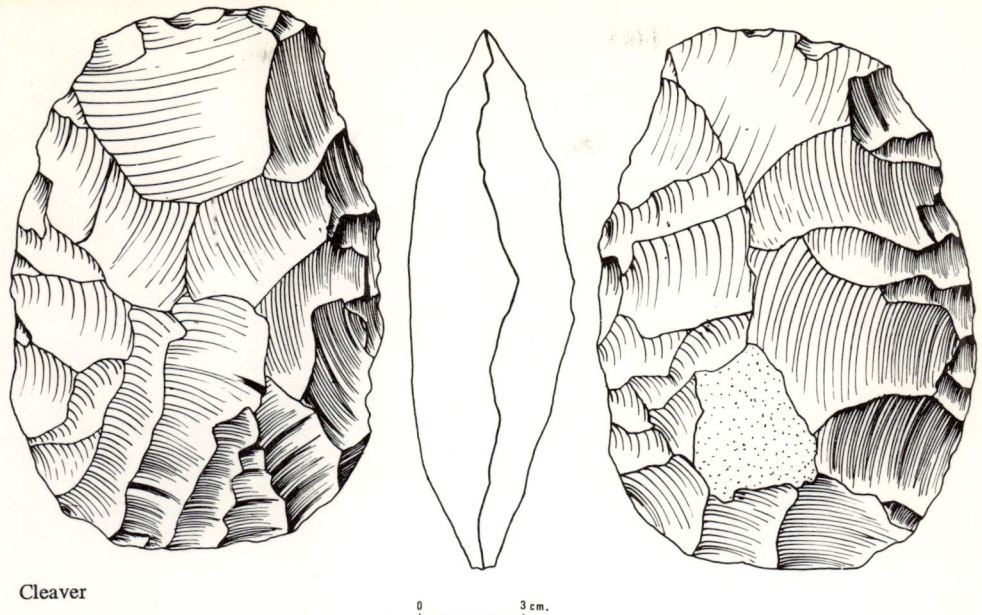

Cleaver

0 _____ 3 cm.

Within the Acheulean cultural phase (one million years or more), technical progress is very clear. In the beginning, handaxes were extremely diverse in form, showing a low degree of standardization. As time went on, however, standardization increased and handaxes were manufactured in well-defined forms. Also the quantity of labour involved in each tool increased with time: less than 10 flake-removals were normally required for the manufacture of a chopping tool; between 10 and 50 for the crudest handaxe and between 100 to 200 flakes or more for a late Acheulean handaxe. The increased labour was not intended solely to make a functionally better tool but aimed at

an aesthetically better achievement as well — we shall come back to this point.

The crude and frequently difficult to define flake tools of the Oldowan culture gradually evolved into more varied and better standardized types during the Acheulean culture. Various scrapers, notches, denticulates*, knives* and awis* can now clearly be identified. Higher standardization of tool manufacture denotes a more precise mental template shared more closely by members of the group, which in its turn denotes a better communication system.

The soft hammer made its appearance early in the course of Acheulean

Left: A horse painted on the wall of the cave of Lascaux, France. Ca. 15,000 years ago

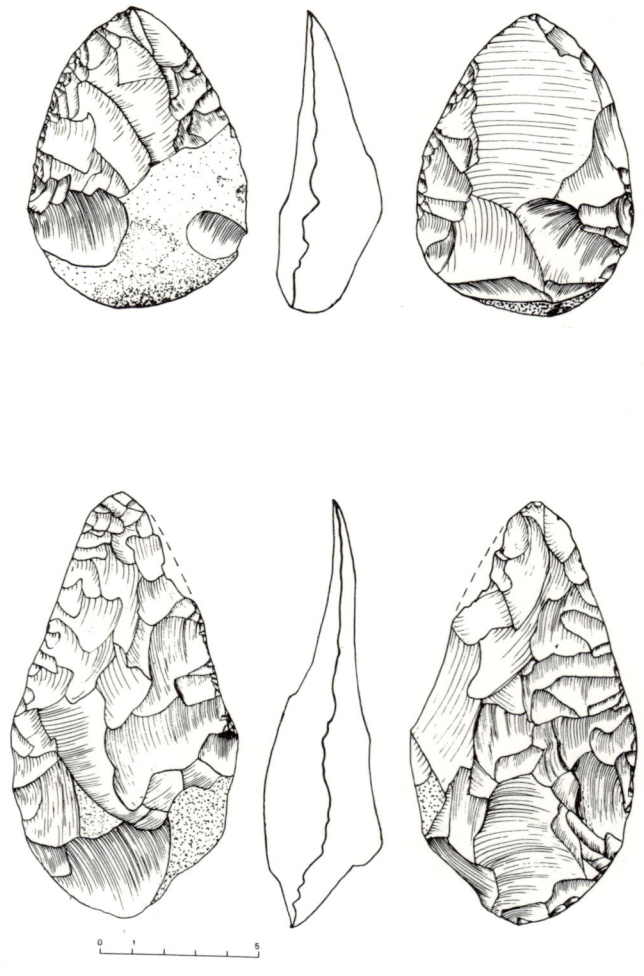

Late Acheulean handaxes

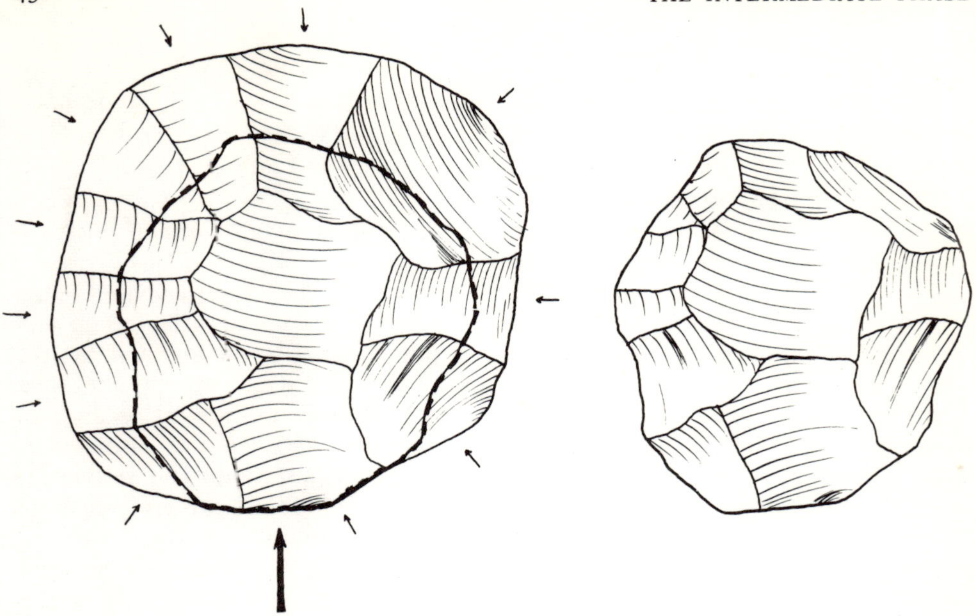

The production of a Levallois flake. (Small arrows indicate preparatory flakes; large arrow, final removal)

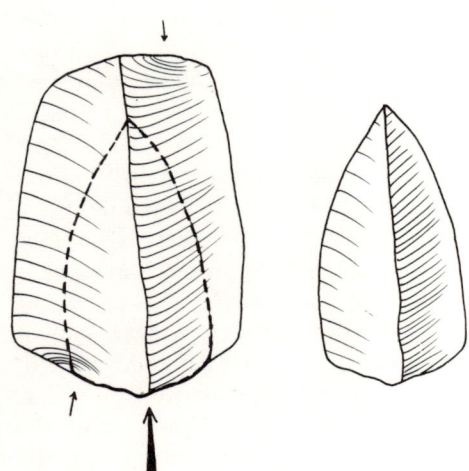

The production of a Levallois point

culture. A blow from a soft hammer (made of wood or antler bone) detached a thinner flake than the stone hammer. Consequently, edges could be more delicately worked and the shape of a tool could thus be better controlled. The soft hammer brought forth an entirely new level of precision in stone knapping. In the Middle Acheulean, the Levallois technique* appeared and in some tool assemblages gained a great importance. This technique consists of flakes and points whose shape was determined by a special preparation prior to their detachment, which discloses a profound knowledge of the physical properties of stone.

These technological traits — new methods of stone-working, higher standardization, a more diverse tool-kit — point to a more skilful man. This man had more to learn than his predecessors and his nervous system had to cope with a greater learning ability and with the greater need for precision. Language consequently had to become more complex. We can safely assume that the more advanced technological complexity of the Acheuleans must reflect also a greater cultural complexity, ranging somewhere between that of initial man and modern man.

It should be emphasized, however, that some human groups of the Intermediate Phase had industries different from the Acheulean. The other industries fall into two major groups: pebble cultures and flake industries. Pebble cultures are Oldowan-like industries where choppers constitute the major element. Flake industries include almost entirely flake tools; handaxes or choppers are rare or altogether absent.

Homo erectus — meaning upright man — appeared roughly at the beginning of the Intermediate Human Phase and is associated with the three major types of industry found during this phase. His cranial capacity reached between 800 and 1200 cc. This type of man is known to have existed throughout the Old World — the Far East, Near East, Africa and Europe.

2. *Subsistence and Behaviour*

Man of the Intermediate Phase maintained essentially the same geographical distribution attained by the late Oldowan stage: Africa, the Near East and the temperate regions of Europe and Asia, perhaps with a more northerly penetration. The settlement patterns denote the same preference for lakes and streams as before, with a restricted use of caves or rock shelters. Very large sites probably signify favourable localities to which people repeatedly returned in the course of their seasonal migrations. Clear cultural differentiation is apparent, as manifested by the three major branches of industries mentioned above: the Acheulean, the pebble cultures and the flake industries. Differences also exist within each of the major branches, as denoted by a special preference for one or another type of tool. The clearest example is the cleaver*, a handaxe with a straight working edge. This tool was known throughout the entire Acheulean world and is normally represented by a few specimens within the handaxes of the assemblage. But in parts of Africa cleavers were particularly favoured, and they may constitute as much as half of all

Area populated between ca. 1 million and ca. 40,000 years ago

the handaxes. A similar tool-kit exists in only a few sites outside Africa, a fact which may indicate new migrating groups.

A striking difference between man of the intermediate phase and man of the initial phase lies in their subsistence patterns, or more precisely, in their respective hunting preferences. During the initial human phase, mainly small animals were hunted, as might indeed be expected considering the natural abilities of man. During the intermediate phase, however, there is a clear shift to big-game hunting. This is best represented by the remains of such huge creatures as the elephant, giraffe, bull and the now-extinct sabre-toothed tiger, giant baboon and giant antelope. Remains of these animals are found either at killing and butchering sites or on living-floors. This raises the question of exactly what took place, since man can hardly be imagined hunting an elephant or tiger without a rifle. Something must have taken place in nature's equilibrium in order to allow a medium-sized creature like man to hunt the most formidable and dangerous animals. Seeking an answer in the archaeological record, we find fire to be the most likely reason for man's new position in nature, a position unequalled by any other animal.

3. *The Manipulation of Fire*

The oldest evidence of fire at a human dwelling hitherto known is about 750,000 years old, and was found in the Escale cave in southern France by E. Bonifay. The use of fire is also attested to the oldest *Homo erectus* layer in Chukution in China. Although it has not yet been accurately dated, this layer is said to be half a million years old or more, within the same time range as the Escale cave. There are difficulties in recognizing the use of fire at ancient sites, because its traces are easily scattered, blown or washed away. A few charred bones or stones at a site cannot be taken as conclusive evidence of the deliberate use of fire, since they could have resulted from accidental fire caused by lightning or volcanic eruption. The oldest recognizable evidence mentioned above (in France and China) is composed of localized ashes which indicate unquestionable man-made fireplaces.

Whether these are really the oldest occurrences we do not know, but at the moment they must be accepted as such. Also, we do not know precisely when the use of fire began in other regions of the world — in Africa, for example, the oldest clear manipulation of fire by man presently known dates only from 55,000 years ago. In view of the European and Asian evidence, this date seems surprisingly recent. We may consider 750,000 years ago to be roughly the start of the use of fire, at least by some human groups.

This achievement marks, in my opinion, the beginning of the intermediate human phase because, for the first time in history, man acquired a technical device achieved by no other animal. Up to that time, man's achievements, spectacular as they may have been, were but a continuation of those of other animals. His tool-kit and behaviour patterns had enabled him to survive and to cope successfully with his environment, the way lions do by means of their own behaviour and organic "tool-kit". The efficiency of both tool-kits could even be compared on a common basis, for example by the number of successful kills per attempt in hunting, or according to the time and energy used in hunting and dismembering one kilogramme of meat. But unlike language or tools, fire was not an extension of anything that existed in the animal world. Rather, it was a revolutionary achievement on a totally different level. A comparison is no longer possible between man and animal.

Theoretically speaking, from this point onwards man ceased to be an object of prey and became solely a hunter — man has definitely acquired an unnatural status. All animals are frightened of fire, so that a fireplace made the safest refuge any living creature ever enjoyed. Also, setting fire to the bush was an excellent way to drive game into a trap. At Torralba, Spain, the remains of a large number of elephants were found at an Acheulean killing-site by Clark Howell.[15] The discoveries suggest that the animals were driven into a swampy area where they sank in the mud and thus could be approached for the kill. It seems as though the animals were forced there by firing the near-by bush. It is indeed probable that big-game hunting would not have been possible at all without the aid of fire.

It is believed by some scholars that man was able to leave Africa to inhabit cooler regions only after fire was mastered. If so, we have indirect evidence of the use of fire both in the earliest settlers outside Africa and in the appearance of regular big-game hunting. Both phenomena seem to have occurred about one million years ago which, in the prehistoric sense, is not far from the oldest recorded evidence of the use of fire (750,000 years ago), as already discussed. Whether this innovation came with *Homo erectus* or

with an earlier type of man we do not know.

When man learned to light a fire, as against manipulating it, is also unknown. It may be assumed that at first natural fire was transported to the site and conserved; records show that even some modern primitives did this. Later, at some unknown date, fire-lighting was invented. But the revolutionary impact of fire upon man is the same. Warmth and security are the most obvious effects. At the same time, fire probably also affected socialization, by getting people together around the hearth. We may assume that the fireplace had become the centre of home activity as well as of cultural activities such as chatting, reciting hunting stories, recalling past experiences and memories of all sorts, thus becoming a centre for adults to exchange information and for the young to absorb it. At some unknown time, miming the hunt or any other moving experience could have been the starting point for drama, chant and dance.

We have already touched upon the most human of all human characteristics — the knowledge of time. In order to recite past experiences one has to be conscious of the past in the first place, and one must be able to distinguish it clearly from the present. Recalling the past is done through words (no matter if spoken or thought), and an elaborate language must have come into use — essentially the language of modern man. With the past and the present, the future was perceived and it became a subject of reflection. Direct evidence for the perception of future, and of time in general, exists in the archaeological record only in the next stage of human development, that of psychologically modern man.

The intermediate phase ends when the concept of time was reached. In my opinion, this was realized through the manipulation of fire. At first glance, the recognition of time may seem a simple matter since so many of nature's phenomena indicate it: sun, moon, stars and seasons of the year. And yet no animal is aware of time. Obviously no animal has begun to observe phenomena that occur repeatedly at regular intervals, then to formulate laws that lead it to comprehend time. Basically, the procedure consists of observing, and being aware of, the presence and absence of a phenomenon: day present — day absent (night), sun present, or absent, and so forth. But think how many elements may be present or absent in nature: besides the sun and the moon there may or may not be hunger, thirst, rain, thunder, the other sex, solar eclipses and death, to name only a few. While some may easily be distinguished as time-factored, most are less clearly so. It is not a simple task to distinguish the few clearly time-denoting phenomena from the many unclear phenomena. And furthermore, why take the trouble of distinguishing and of law-making? Why be aware of these phenomena at all? These things are there, they simply happen to be and if they are not, well, the world is complicated. I am trying here to explain the animal way of reasoning, and I feel that man was naturally inclined to reason in a similar way. What is indeed surprising is that after man and baboon have spent an equal length of time regarding nature, man knows that the year 1900 has passed and will not return, but the baboon does not.

The knowledge of time is not innate. Man is not born with it — he learns it. *Something* had to provoke him to become aware of the simple (and at the same time so complicated) matter of absence and presence, and this brings us back to fire.

When conquered, fire became the first matter whose absence or presence could be controlled by man. Of all nature's processes, it was the only one which was reversible by man; he could bring it to life and extinguish it at will. All other processes were non-reversible; a slaughtered animal or a dead fellow man could never be brought to life again. Death had of course occurred ever since life existed, but it in itself implied nothing to arouse a greater concern on the part of man than it had among chimpanzees. The same is true for any other natural phenomenon of absence-presence, of which life and death are the most striking example (even affecting animals, to some extent). Thus, the natural phenomena, whether time-factored or not, would not normally attract attention or require explanation. But fire was beyond the normal phenomena in that it could be revived at will. Furthermore, fire is easily conceived as a living being and was probably taken as such by ancient man; it moves, eats, makes sounds and heats. All over the world similar words applied to fire and events of death and life attest to this basic attitude.

Not only did fire behave in a way no other phenomenon did; the very social position of man changed through the use of fire, as we have already noted. From an equal member in the natural world who, like the others, hunted and was hunted, man became 'supernatural' in the sense that he became an almighty hunter who practically could not be hunted. Man became, in Margalef's words, a "historical accident, comparable to the development of trees with almost indigestible trunks".[16] Once conceived of, this situation too gave food for thought.

Our opinion is that man's manipulation of fire changed his way of thinking from that of an animal and aroused his concern about phenomena which had always existed, but were never thought about before. Fire allowed man to become a creator, and only a creator is concerned with creation.

4. *Degree of Humanization*

The intermediate phase began with the mastering of fire, the technical achievement that definitely separated man from the animal world perhaps one million years ago. What caused this achievement? We can only guess. We know that man had gradually lost his covering of hair, but not when this took place. Maybe fire came as a response to this, or perhaps as a response to the onset of a glacial period, or to the necessity of migrating to cooler regions. Be that as it may, the stimulus had to be strong enough for man to overcome the deeply rooted fear of fire. Thus, from its very beginning, fire must have involved not merely a technical innovation but a psychological adaption as well.

During the intermediate human phase the psycho-social traits of man evolved, apparently stemming from the manipulation of fire. At the end of the process, man emerged as the being now known to us: he fears death and is hence restless, he seeks explanation and hence explores. The aesthetic and scientific achievements of modern man stem from this state of mind. When was the new state of mind achieved? It appears in the archaeological record about 100,000 years ago with the wide-scale appearance of objects of a clearly aesthetic persuasion, and about 70,000 years ago with the first appearance of burials.

This range of time marks for us the end of the intermediate phase and the onset of the last phase — that of full humanity.

VI   FULLY HUMAN

Each of several occurrences can be taken to mark the beginning of the fully human phase. As was the case with the intermediate and initial phases, we are dealing here as well with a process and not with a single event. Nevertheless, archaeologists chose one specific event for the sake of convenience. The first appearance of burials some 70,000 years ago indicates definitely that a fully human mind was reached. This date may be taken as the beginning of the last phase of human history. However, some indications exist which hint at an even earlier attainment of this state. These are of an aesthetic order, which as we believe could not have existed before the knowledge of time and death was reached. In the late Acheulean, around 100,000 years ago, many hand-axes frequently show an extremely precise and symmetric shape, involving a delicate workmanship and an amount of labour that seems excessive for the achievement of functional purposes alone. Hence, a desire for perfection and beauty is felt in these tools. Striving for perfection is believed to result from a fear of death and concern with what will be left behind when one dies. No such motivation is known among animals, as they do not seem to know of death and hence do not fear it.

Another piece of evidence which has recently come to light, and which may possibly indicate a fully human mind, takes us back to about 130,000 years ago. It is an engraved bone which was recently unearthed in an Acheulean layer at Combe Grenal in France by F. Bordes.[17] Microscopic examination by A. Marschack has shown it to be purposely engraved. This unique object is the oldest artistic manifestation known at present.

1.   The Knowledge of Death

The end of the intermediate human phase coincides with that of the Lower Palaeolithic period in common prehistoric terminology. The fully human phase embraces, in the same terminology, the Middle Palaeolithic, the

The oldest human artistic expression, an engraved bone ca. 150,000 years old (Pech de l'Azé, France. Excavation F. Bordes)

Upper Palaeolithic and the post-Palae-olithic (Holocene). This division will be followed henceforth.

The most striking characteristic of the Middle Palaeolithic, from our point of view, is the worldwide appearance of burials. They consisted of a grave cut at the place of habitation — a cave or rock shelter — into which the corpse was placed in a flexed position; arms and legs bent into what looks like a foetal position. Grave goods were then placed with the dead: tools, remains of food and animal horns have been found alongside the skeletons in various graves. In the Shanidar cave in Iraq, ex-cavated by R. Solecki, flowers were also placed in the grave, as evidenced by the remaining pollen.[18] In some cases stone slabs were placed on the corpse. Finally, the grave and its con-tents were covered with earth and sometimes the whole was spread with red ochre. From the very beginning, burial customs point to a complex ritual or ceremony whose basic con-cepts seem to indicate a respect for the dead, a wish to appease and a belief in a

A burial ca. 45,000 years old. Note the flexed position of the body (Cave of Skhul, Israel. Excavation McCown)

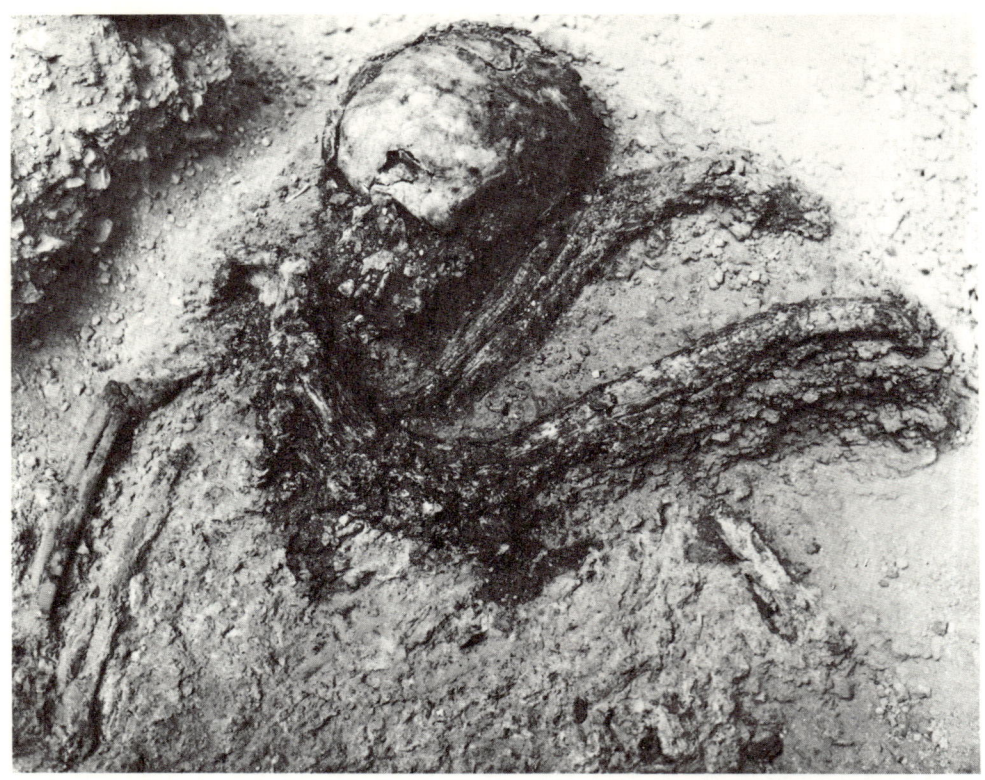

An adolescent's burial with antlers, perhaps 50,000 years old (Cave of Qafza, Israel. Excavation Vandermeersch)

continued existence after death. Man has held sacred the same basic concepts ever since.

2. *Subsistence and Culture*

The oldest burials show man with a cranial capacity equal to ours, approxi- mately 1,500 cc. This essentially modern man is called early *Homo sapiens* (or *Homo sapiens neander- thalensis,* his full name). He preferred caves and rock shelters for dwelling sites wherever available. This is thought to be connected with the cold period in which early *Homo sapiens* is known to have lived, during the early half of the last Glacial period. At the same time, however, these men dwelt in open areas as well. They penetrated into regions farther north than did their predecessors, thus showing a better ability to cope with colder conditions: a dwelling made of animal skins has been found in the Russian plain, and it is assumed that hide clothing was also one of the adaptive devices, although none has survived from this period.

Except for colouring material such as ochre or manganese with which body paintings are assumed to have been drawn, no objects of art have survived among early *Homo sapiens* cultural remains.

The Middle Palaeolithic stone industry that followed the Acheulean shows a greater cultural diversity than formerly. The basic tool-kit was made of flakes and was the continuation of the Acheulean flake-tool component. Handaxes were no longer manufactured by most Middle Palaeolithic cultures, but several continued to fabricate and utilize them. To the basic Acheulean flake tools such as scrapers, notches and denticulates, several new tools were added: characteristic implements now are the Mousterian point*, the leaf-shaped point* and Emira points*. Cultural units were manifested in more limited geographical areas than before. For example, the leaf-shaped point

characterizes the Central European industries while the Emira point characterizes those of the Near East. At the same time, different industries also co-existed within each of the major cultural areas. This heterogeneity may be interpreted as various tribal traditions or as tool-kits variously intended for different activities. Stone tool technology was the same as that developed previously, with both hard and soft hammers used and with the Levallois technique preponderant in some assemblages and absent in others.

Early modern man did not use hunting methods which differed from those of his predecessors, except that he may have been more efficient in hafting stone tools onto the tip of a wooden handle. This seems to have been the purpose of the diverse points that were added in great quantities to the former tool-kit. In some cases, there seemed to be a reliance on a single species of animal as the main source of meat supply: deer, horse and cattle are recorded in this connection, depending on the type of environment. Man's reliance on and exploitation of herd animals have been taken to suggest that some kind of a symbiosis existed between them, which may have evolved later into domestication.

Some 40,000 years ago, with the onset of the second half of the last European Glacial period, important cul-

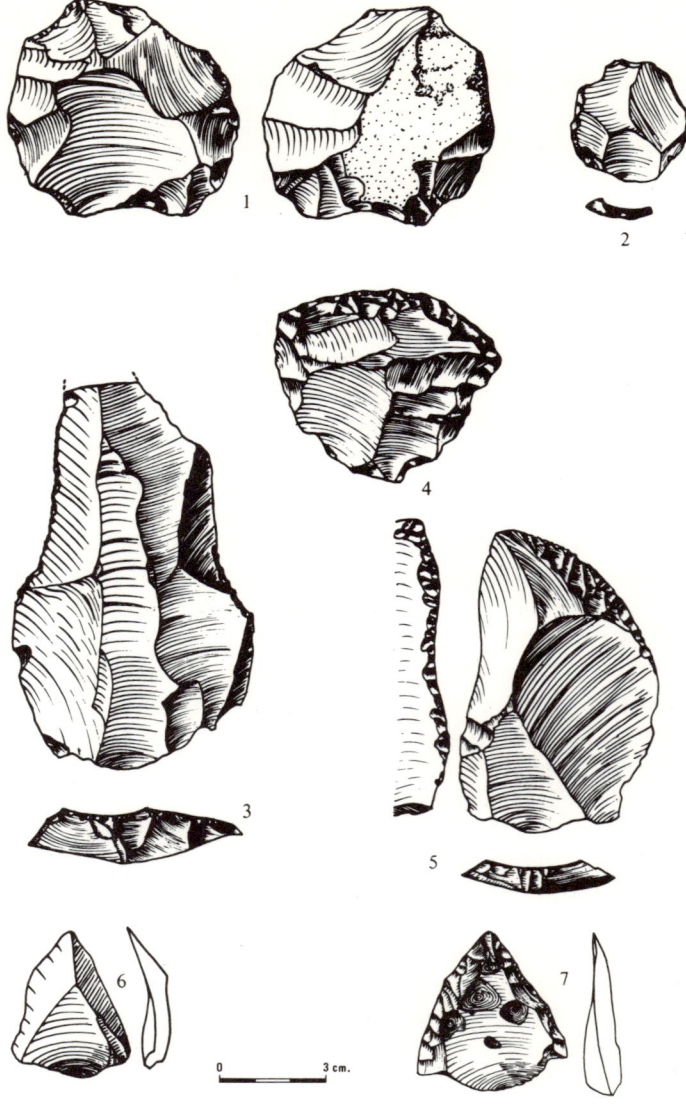

Middle Palaeolithic tools. 1 – Levallois core. 2, 3 – Levallois flakes. 4, 5 – Scrapers. 6 – Levallois point. 7 – Mousterian point (with cavities produced by heat fractures)

tural changes marked the end of the Middle Palaeolithic and the beginning of the Upper Palaeolithic phase.

3. *Man and Arts*

Until not long ago, the cultural shift from the Middle to Upper Palaeolithic was considered the best example of a direct relation between a certain human type and a definite culture. The shift seemed to have coincided with the extinction of *Homo sapiens neanderthalensis* and his replacement by *Homo sapiens sapiens.* In recent years it has been clearly shown that *Homo sapiens sapiens* had co-existed during the Middle Palaeolithic with the Neanderthal, and both were associated with the same Middle Palaeolithic stone industry.

The Upper Palaeolithic is marked above all by the first abundant appearance of arts: rock-paintings, sculptures, engravings and ornaments suddenly flourished. The themes used in Upper Palaeolithic art are animals, human figures, plants and symbolic notations. In a recent study by A. Marshack,[19] certain notations were suggested to be lunar calendars. If this interpretation is correct, then we have the oldest direct evidence of the knowledge of time. (Other notations are as yet undeciphered.) A concern with time, or a time-factored mind, is also expressed in numerous works of art where particular themes depict certain seasons of the year: for example animals in heat, pregnant animals, the migration of herds, plants in blossom and other illustrated observations. Figurines of women or animals, sculptured from or engraved in ivory, bone, stone and even burnt clay, seem to be personal or family objects. The repeated occurrences of the female body, with well developed feminine organs and a schematic rendering of other traits, suggests that women were already considered mysterious and powerful because of their ability to give life and hence their potential for doing evil. These prehistoric "Venuses" have been alternatively interpreted as fertility-symbols and witches.

In addition to those aspects of modern human culture — burials and arts — that are fully evidenced in the Upper Palaeolithic, we may assume a basically modern pattern for other cultural aspects that cannot be directly inferred from existing remains. Institutions, for example, seem to have formalized behaviour to a point where individuality was emphasized by personal adornments which appear in quantity for the first time. Possibly the concern with life, death, fertility and cosmological phenomena added up to a set philosophy or religion.

Indications for the existence of ceremonies appear both in burials and in

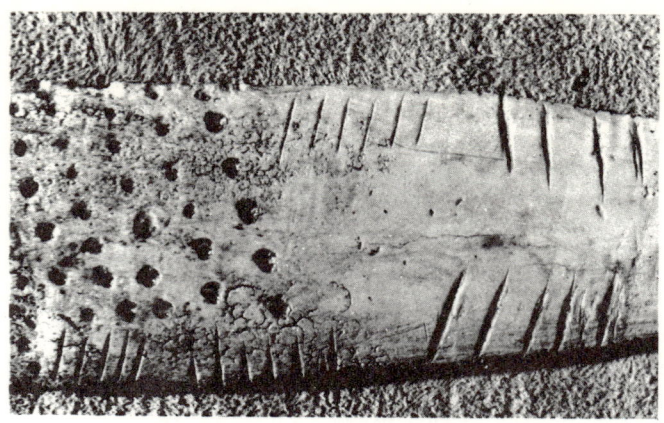

Indentations engraved in bone. Note the grouping of forms and the different pressures applied. From Lartet, France, ca. 32,000 years ago (Microscopic photography by A. Marshack)

The oldest known sculpture of human body (female, with animal's head), carved in bone, 32,000 years old (Hohlenstein-Stadel, Germany)

Women apparently performing a dance. Note garments and the infant attached to the back of one. Engraving on stone (Gonnersdorf, Germany, Excavation Bosihski.) 12,500 years ago.

cave art. We may assume that ceremonies centred around calendar events (completion of a migration cycle, opening of the hunting or fishing season, and so on) as well as personal events (birth, initiation and death).

The more we know about Upper Palaeolithic man, the more like modern primitives and ourselves he seems. These advanced hunter-gatherers were able to express ideas so clearly through art that most probably they could also express and communicate thoughts by the use of language as accurately as we can today. Their notations must have depicted events, situations or ideas that were understood at least by some of the group if not by all, hence they truly constitute a system of written communication. The potential for pictographic writing existed, then, from the

"Venus" from Dolni-Vestonice, Czechoslovakia. Ca. 25,000 years ago beginning of the Upper Palaeolithic, to become realized when conditions made it necessary. Our present idea of when such conditions first occurred (*ca.* 5000 BC) may yet have to be modified.

4. *Subsistence and Culture*

Upper Palaeolithic stone industry discloses major changes from the preceding Middle Palaeolithic technology. Some common, world-wide traits now appeared together with an increasing cultural specialization by cultural provinces which continuously grew smaller in size.

The common world-wide traits are both technical and typological. Technically, the old-established method of a direct blow by a hammer now changed into an indirect one. In other words, a punch was introduced between the core to be struck and the hammer. The punch, probably made of antler or some other hard substance, allowed a greater precision than before, because the position and angle of the blow could now be more accurately determined. Flakes removed by the punch technique can be distinguished by the small protuberance of their bulb of percussion. This technique enabled man to strike finer and longer flakes, which are termed blades.

Another technical improvement

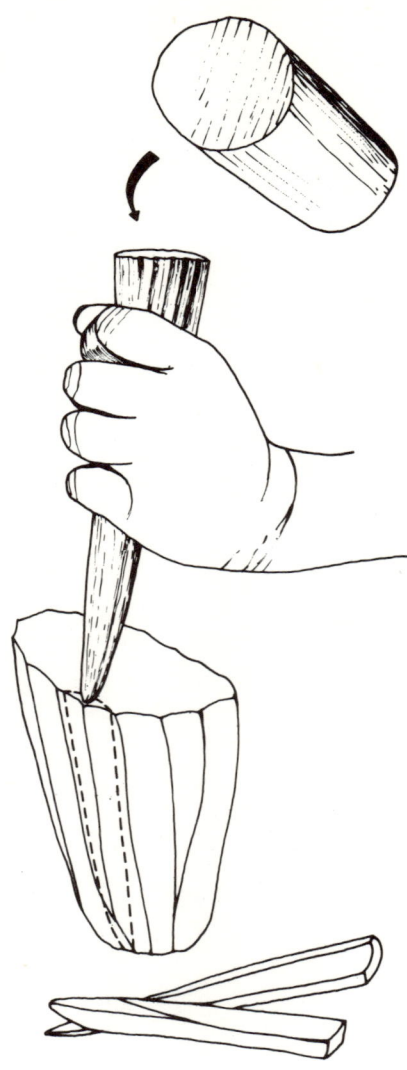

Detaching blades with a punch

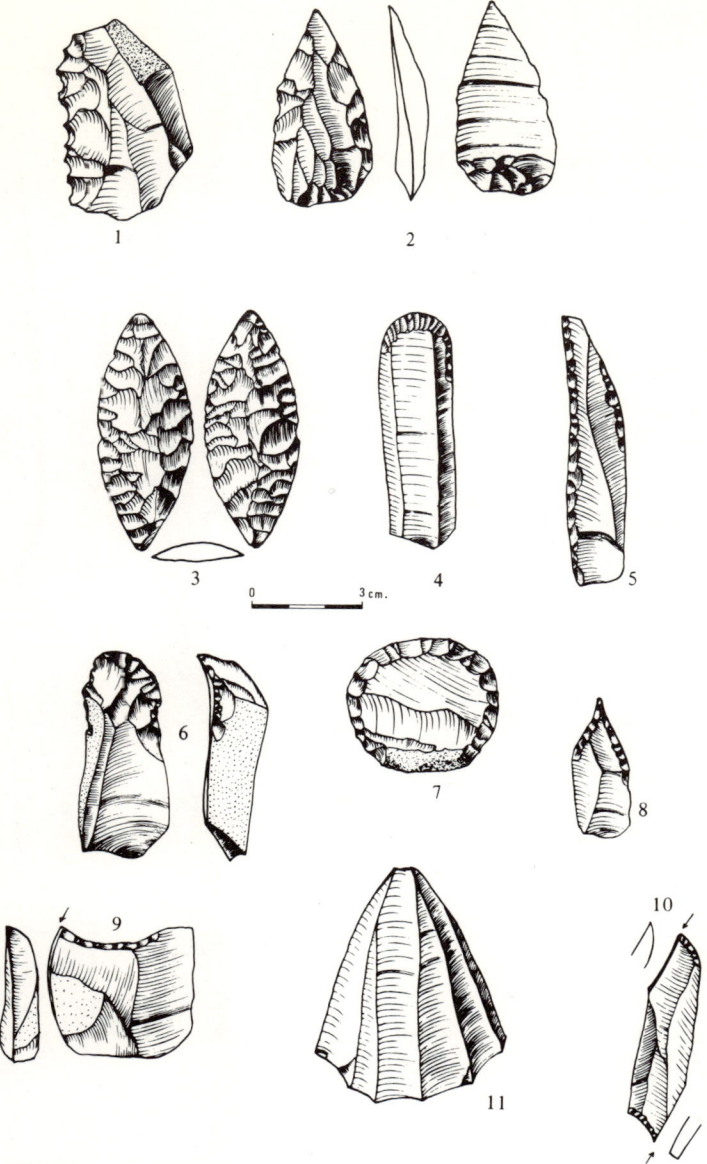

Upper Palaeolithic tools. 1 — Denticulate. 2, 3 — Points. 4–7 — Scrapers. 8 — Awl. 9, 10 — Burins. 11 — Blade core

helped further to increase the precision of stone working — the discovery that heating flint-stone renders it much easier to shape by retouch, without altering its hardness. Flakes and blades which underwent heating were best suited to pressure-retouching, which consisted of pressing on the flake's edge, instead of the usual striking. Using the combined method of heating and pressure-flaking, the most perfect stone tools in prehistory were manufactured, especially projectile-points.

The Upper Palaeolithic tool-kit was more diverse than that of the Middle Palaeolithic, the characteristic tools were end-scrapers* and burins* (or gravers). Burins are believed to have been connected with precision work in wood, bone or stone, as reflected by the objects of art and the many bone tools which were made at that time.

During the Upper Palaeolithic human population spread, for the first time, all over the world; the American and Australian continents were inhabited by migrations from Asia. The oldest human remains in Australia date from about 30,000 years ago, while the date of the first migration to the New World is still unclear. It is clear, however, that several waves of migration reached the New World across the Bering Strait.

Life in such varied environments and climates as offered by the earth requires a rich variety of adaptations and

0   3 cm.

Harpoon and spear-points of bone

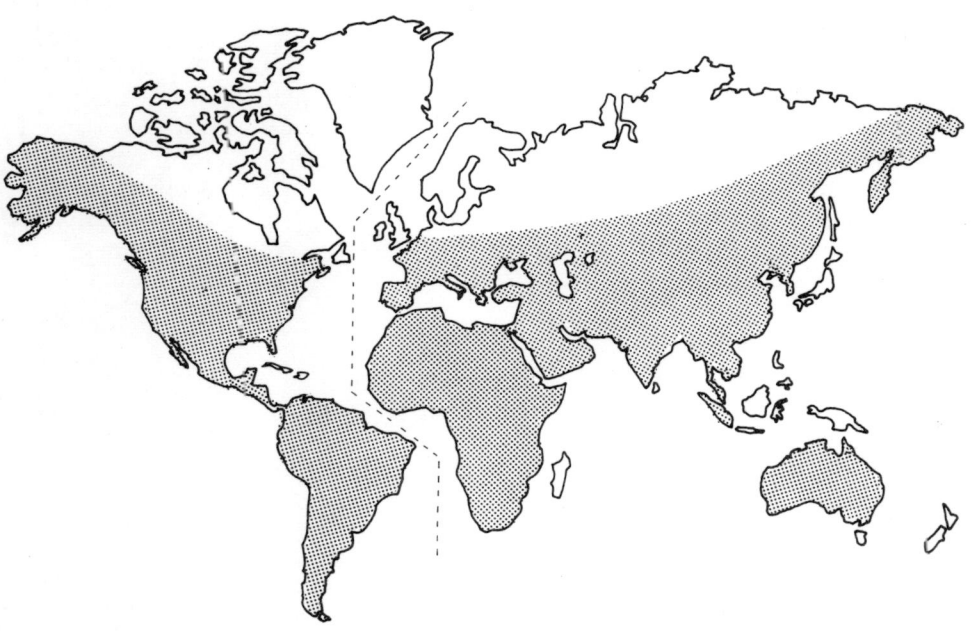

Area populated during Upper Palaeolithic between ca. 35,000 and 20,000 years ago

subsistence strategies. Indeed, these are seen in the archaeological record through the increased number of regional cultures in the Upper Palaeolithic, and especially in its latter phase when cultural zones were frequently reduced to the size of modern countries or even smaller. Since cultural variations occurred also within a uniform climatic region, it means that the rate of change of cultural adaptations exceeded the rate of idea spreading.

The basic methods of subsistence remained as before. But the great variety of bone tools and projectile points, constituting an important and characteristic part of Upper Palaeolithic assemblages, indicate an improvement in hunting technique. A major improvement was the invention of the spear-thrower which, by increasing the leverage of the human arm, became the first efficient propulsive device invented by man and the most effective weapon preceding the bow and arrow.

The dependence on practically one single species of animal for food is even more striking now than before. Hunters living in the open and cold Eurasian plains consumed mammoths almost exclusively. Numerous dwellings built of animal hides were left by these hunters. In more temperate areas, reindeer constituted the major staple food. The same dependence is seen in the New World where variously mammoth, bison or horse were hunted. The life of these advanced hunters must have been centred around the herd or herds they exploited. The seasonal migration patterns of the animals conditioned, to a large extent, man's own behaviour.

The transition from hunting-gathering to the domestication of plants and animals took place in the last millennia of the Palaeolithic period — termed the Epi-Palaeolithic. During this period, then, the foundations for our present-day patterns of living were laid. In spite of long and tedious research, no conditions appear during this period that could clearly account for the move towards domestication. Rather, the move seems to have been initiated by factors existing long before, and by pressure which built up extremely gradually, pressure which had to do with the subsistence patterns of man long before domestication became necessary.

The reader will remember that man broke away from a pure equilibrium with nature roughly a million years ago, with the capture of fire. The pre-fire, or the animal patterns of subsistence, were completely governed by equilibrated relations of prey-predator. The number of a given species cannot appreciably exceed the quantity of its food supply,

and the limit actually lies well below the potential food supply. When this threshold is exceeded, various mechanisms regulate a decrease in the number of the species. These mechanisms are not yet fully understood, but they involve bio-chemical processes which govern reproduction. Thus, an animal can normally multiply only if its food supply multiplies, which in turn depends on another food supply, and so on. All the factors of the entire ecosystem thus react upon each other. This occurs normally, but man was not to conform to the norm after his acquisition of fire. As we have seen, fire turned man into a formidable predator who practically ceased to be a prey. Thus, the major factor which normally maintains population stability no longer applied to man. Fire, furthermore, would have meant the killing of many more animals than man needed for food — for example, when hunting through firing a large bush area was practised. This new technique and a steadily growing human population inevitably caused increased pressure upon food sources.

The archaeological fact which best reveals this pressure is the extinction of various animal species during the Palaeolithic period. Once believed to have resulted solely from natural causes (for example, climatic changes), Palaeolithic extinctions are now considered by certain scientists to have been caused mostly by man.[20] In addition, a food-supply species does not have to become extinct in order to cause stress; enough is caused if the supply is rare. Among the facts that are impossible to extract from the archaeological record is precisely this information: how long did man have to hunt for the animal whose bones we find in his refuse? In other words, how abundant was the prey in any given area and period of time?

A similar pressure must have been put on vegetable food since, as mankind increased in number, berries and nuts became relatively scarcer.

One of man's responses to such stress would have been the widening of his living territory. Indeed, this is very clearly shown in the archaeological record with man's gradual conquering of the entire world. Another response to deteriorating resources is better methods of their exploitation: better organization, better co-operation and more efficient tools, all of which are

amply evidenced throughout prehistory. The continuous deterioration of the environment may in fact have had a share in man's growing anxiety, one which led to his concern with death and religion. Artistic expressions may have originated as yet another means of coping with scarcity; supernatural help is particularly relied upon in situations of stress.

The potential to domesticate had always existed; man had lived amidst plants and animals for a very long time, and he knew their ways perfectly well. But conditions had to occur which would motivate realization of the potential. These conditions are not to be sought only in the Epi-Palaeolithic when man was finally led to domesticate. Rather, it was the culmination of the steadily mounting ecological deterioration caused, in the first place, by man himself.

1. *Subsistence and Culture*

The right conditions for domestication did not occur simultaneously in all parts of the world; in fact, in some areas they do not exist even today. In the Epi-Palaeolithic, every human group coped with the crisis in its own way, as environment and the circumstances permitted. There appears to have been a worldwide refinement and complication of stone industries with

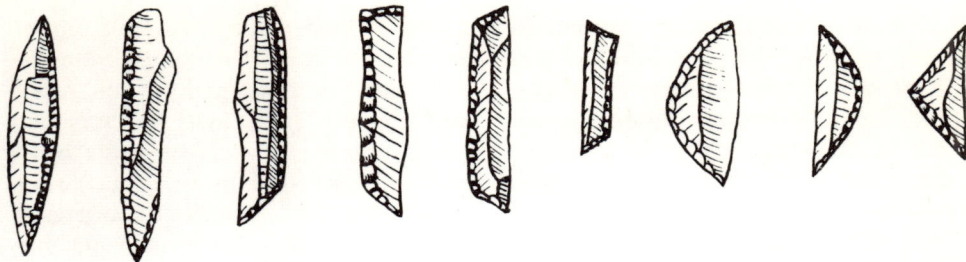

Tiny stone tools (microliths) which characterize the Epi-Palaeolithic

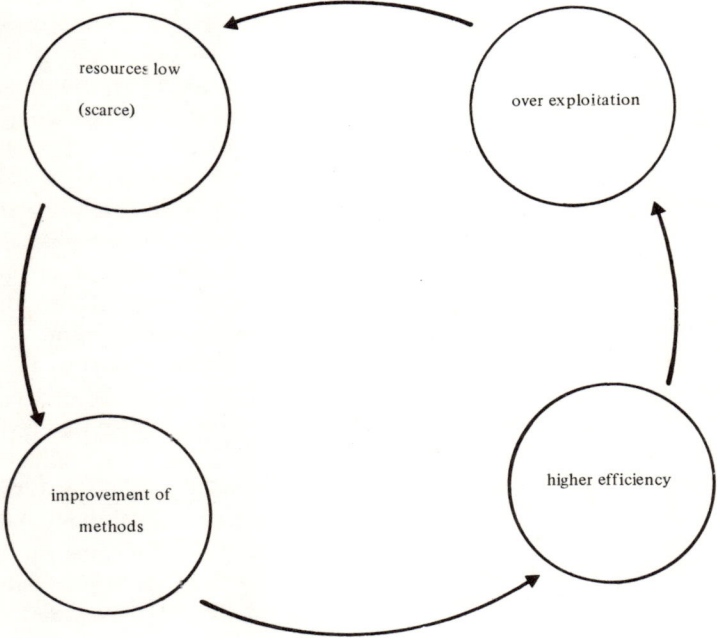

Diagram to show circular relationship between the environment and its exploitation

the massive introduction of micro-liths*, or tiny stone tools. Normally less than two centimetres in length, these were laboriously inserted into wood or bone points to form composite and more efficient tools. The absence of microliths in the New World is instructive, since it may denote that this relatively newly occupied land was as yet less subjected to human destructive subsistence patterns than the Old World, and hence the need for a refined technology was not felt. The stress was to come in the New World as well, and domestication was to appear slightly later in time.

A complex technology and, seemingly, a complex level of social organization, are required in order to best exploit the greatest possible variety of food resources. This is precisely what we see in the Epi-Palaeolithic, when man made use of the widest range of resources ever documented: besides the traditional collecting and hunting, shell-fish and landsnails were consumed in huge quantities; fishing must have acquired a hitherto unknown importance, since special implements for fishing now made their first appearance. The bow and arrow may also have been invented during the Epi-Palae-olithic — a better tool for the hunting of scarcer game.

At present, the oldest archaeological evidence known which directly denotes a strong reliance upon vegetable food — presumably cereals — comes from the Near East. Here, around the wild cereal belt, appear the oldest mortars and pestles intended for cereal (and acorn?) grinding. According to radiocarbon dating, this invention came about some 15,000 years ago. While small and shallow mortars for colour grinding are known prior to this date, the new deep mortars were introduced later everywhere agriculture was practised. Now, there is no reason to suppose that wild cereals, or acorns, were not always consumed. But the invention of a special tool for these foods denotes, as with all other inventions, the growing importance of the need for which the new implement was designed. It is yet unclear if these people simply consumed wild grains, or were growing them already. In our opinion, the invention of grinding tools marks the beginning of the process of domestication.

The most ancient mortars have been found in Israel; they formed part of a microlithic stone industry at a site near the Sea of Galilee[21] and in another on the coastal plain. They are made of basalt, which is an extremely hard rock to hollow out. In this same time period there appears a dense human habitation along the eastern Mediterranean, manifested by a large number of sites, some of which exceed 2000 square metres in area. Normally no architecture is evi-

Oldest deep mortar and its pestle, made of basalt, 15,000 years old (Ein-Gev, Israel. Excavation Bar-Yosef)

dent, but in one case an agglomeration of circular stone structures was found which may possibly be referred to as a "village". Both the abundance of Epi-Palaeolithic sites and their size are a direct contradiction to the preceding Upper Palaeolithic period along the eastern Mediterranean, where only a few rather small sites are known. Thus it appears that a considerable increase in population occurred in the east Mediterranean which gave rise to the first groups of circular structures and the first grinding tools — or the onset of domestication.

Some three thousand years later, sickle blades* are added in substantial numbers to the tool kit, a further indication of the importance cereals attained. Sickle blades were made of flint and were inserted, in a row, into handles of wood or bone. These blades have a characteristic sheen along their cutting edges, which results from repeated rubbing against cereal stalks, which are rich in silica. A similar sheen on stone implements is unknown prior to the appearance of sickle blades about 12,000 years ago, hence we know that the task for which sickle blades were designed was not hitherto performed by any other tool.

Shortly thereafter, the oldest evidence for true domestication is seen, when cereals and wild goats or sheep were transported by man away from

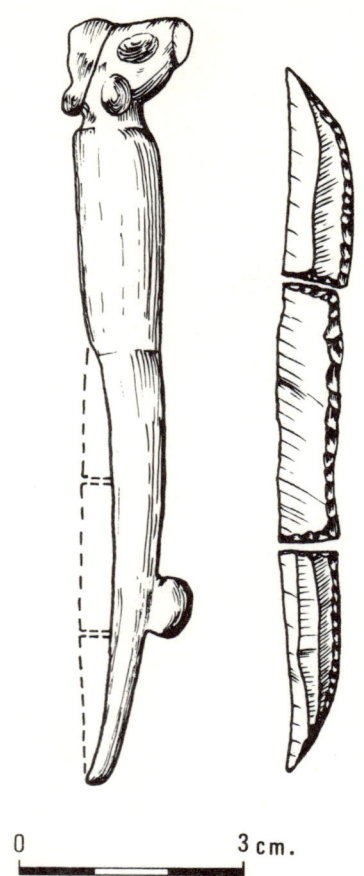

0   3 cm.

Flint sickle-blades and a decorated bone handle

their natural habitat. This phenomenon was reported in Persia and near the Dead Sea approximately 10,000 years ago, and slightly later on the Anatolian plateau. Domestication seems an appropriate term to designate the transplantation of these species, regardless of whether the species involved already acquired the characteristic changes from their wild ancestors, which domestication finally brought about. These changes appear, in fact, for the first time some 8000 to 9000 years ago, at the onset of the Holocene era. At this time the principal domestic crops — wheat and barley in the Near East and the Balkans, rice in the Far East and, perhaps somewhat later, maize in the New World — are clearly distinguished from their respective wild species. The main animals domesticated, and equally distinct from their wild forms, are goats, sheep, pigs, cattle and dogs. The genetic changes domestication entailed could have resulted from deliberate cross-breeding by man, or as an automatic response to the new conditions affected upon them by their captors.[22]

The term "Agricultural revolution" thus designates a process which lasted for at least 7000 years: from the appearance of grinding tools 15,000 years ago to the emergence of fully domesticated forms some 8000 years ago. Plant and animal domestication is in reality a smooth continuation of the peculiar human subsistence pattern which started with the domestication of fire. Ever since that time man no longer adapts passively, as do animals; rather, he adapts actively through an improved exploitation and a continuous devastation of his environment. At first with

THE PROCESS OF DOMESTICATION

	Culture	Years Before Present	Major Stages
HOLOCENE	Metal	present —	Industrial Revolution
		2000 —	
		4000 —	
		6000 —	Written documents
	Neolithic	8000 —	Domesticated forms of food species
		10000 —	Cities
PLEISTOCENE	Epi-Palaeolithic		Transplantation of wild food species
		12000 —	Year-round villages
		14000 —	Sickle-blades
		16000 —	Grinding tools
	Upper Palaeolithic	18000 —	Hunting-gathering

little impact, a gradual and ever-growing stress was placed on the environment by the use of more sophisticated methods of exploiting it. The greater the pressure the greater the scarcity until, with plant and animal domestication, the heaviest stress ever exercised was put on the surface of Earth. Even though the process of domestication finally resulted, as we shall see, in a novelty that changed the world, the people involved in any one stage of that process were probably entirely unaware of it.

2. *The Consequences of Domestication*

The replacement of a hunting-gathering way of life by plant and animal domestication had a profound impact on human behaviour and values, which we shall now consider.

With the practice of plant and animal husbandry, security depended entirely upon amassing and storing wealth — whether grain, animals or land. Large-scale accumulation of wealth, both impossible and unnecessary at a hunter-gatherer level of subsistence, came to constitute a vital necessity in the final stage of the Palaeolithic, when indeed the first granaries or storage places appeared.

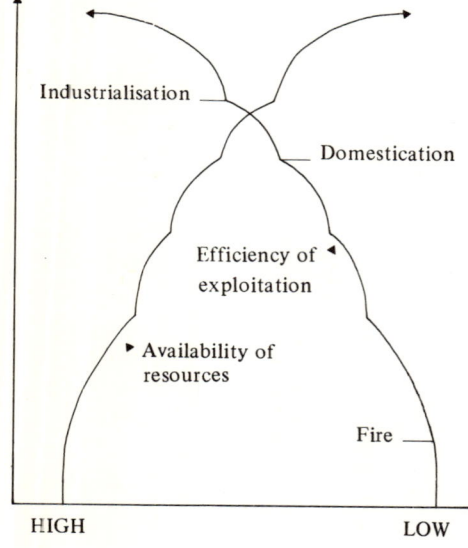

Diagram illustrating the interchange through time between nature's resources and man's efficiency in their exploitation. Each major technical innovation has a strong impact.

Right: A bison engraved in bone from La Madeleine, France, ca. 15,000 years ago

Overleaf left: Sculptured and decorated objects of amber, ca. 10,000 years ago

Overleaf right: Stonehenge, England, a huge astronomical observatory, ca. 5,000 years old

Man's estimation of land probably underwent the most extreme changes. At the hunter-gatherer stage, almost the entire land could have been exploited, with each ecological zone (mountains, lowland, etcetera) contributing its specialties to the total food supply. With the shift to crop growing, only a much smaller portion of the land could be utilized: mountains, forests and rocky terrain were excluded. But later on, when agriculture became dependent upon irrigation, of all the land only the narrow strips along river-banks became utilizable. This drastic reduction of the principal subsistence zone brought about an enormous population density in limited areas; this, together with the need for large-scale storage of goods gave rise to permanent villages and later on to urbanization. Ever since that abrupt reduction of living area to agriculturally fertile land, land has remained our most valued possession.

The view held in the past was that the shift in the subsistence pattern from hunting-gathering to domestication increased security and relieved man of constant worry about the unreliable food supply that hunting would have constituted. According to the same view farmers were assumed to enjoy a greater amount of leisure, which in turn would allow for more creative activities than hunters could experience. However, recent research

Left: A pictographic inscription from Mesopotamia, ca. 5,500 years old

into the economy of modern hunter-gatherers has shown the reverse to be true.[23] Thus, for example, the Bushmen hunter-gatherers, even though forced into an unfavourable region on the fringes of the Kalahari Desert, were better off than their neighbours the Hadza, who practised agriculture. It was the Hadza who, during years of bad crops, entered Bushman territory to forage — not the other way round. Also, hunters were shown to devote much less time to procuring food and hence were able to enjoy more leisure-time than primitive farmers.

These observations lead one to re-examine the long-prevailing glorification of the domesticator as a "creator of food", as against the hunter, whose activities were considered to be "merely devastating". In truth, domestication actually devastates to an unprecedented degree by completely altering natural vegetation and animal life, which led to the ecological problems presently faced by our food-producing society.

3. *Urbanization*

Beginning about 12,000 years ago, there appeared in the Near East, between the Mediterranean and the Euphrates, important agglomerations of circular structures which seem to have been occupied all year round. Several

Circular structures in a village, 12,000 years old (Eynan, Israel. Excavation Perrot)

facts point to this conclusion: along with a microlithic tool kit essentially the same as before, several heavy items are now added which could not easily be carried about. These are stone bowls and large mortars often weighing fifty kilogrammes, which of course rendered them useless to a frequently moving group of people. Another indication of long and steady habitation is indicated by constructed storage pits of granaries, sometimes plastered and sometimes lined with stones to keep the interiors dry. A further indication is graveyards with up to a hundred burials which accompany these Epi-Palaeolithic settlements, whereas in earlier burial places ten skeletons are exceptional. It is perfectly possible that year-round settlements could have existed in some areas prior to this time, under exceptionally favourable conditions. But such sites would invariably have been inhabited by small groups. Only with domestication could a large group live together continuously, with the varied and multiple interactions implied by such a situation.

In the graveyards of the Epi-Palaeolithic, social stratification is disclosed for the first time by an uneven distribution of grave goods. Certain persons were adorned with elaborate ornaments (or signs of status?) which others lack — apparently some people were more highly thought of than others. It is probably correct to assume that the social organization of the villages attained a greater complexity than hitherto; the old way of maintaining daily life, adequate for a small group of family members with a narrow range of subsistence activities, no longer sufficed for villages whose inhabitants may have numbered 200 or more. Furthermore, co-operation in daily life is not as vital for domesticators as it is for hunters. New institutions were required in order to maintain inter- and intra-group relations and to co-ordinate the more varied subsistence activities. Certain persons must have assumed responsibilities vital to the welfare of the group, and they naturally acquired a special status.

The sedentary way of life, the concentration of villages in limited, agriculturally favourable areas and the possibility herein for the exchange of goods brought about conditions wherein permanent market places could have been established, and from which cities would subsequently have emerged.

The world's oldest known cities are Jericho,[24] in Israel, built about 10,000 years ago and Çatal Hüyuk in Anatolia, established 9000 years ago.[25] The better documented example is Çatal Hüyuk, which was a commercial and religious centre. Over a third of the structures uncovered are temples, with the bull apparently the main religious

symbol — perhaps the city-god. Çatal Hüyuk is located near a source of obsidian, a volcanic glass-like rock widely traded as a valuable raw material for tool-making. The city perhaps evolved as a trading centre where farmers, shepherds, hunters and merchants exchanged goods. The trading centre then became a religious one. Large religious centres may have come about as a means for strengthening intra-tribal solidarity and uniting several villages into a larger frame of social organization, than before.[26]

An Epi-Palaeolithic burial with ornaments, ca. 12,000 years old (El-Wad, Israel. Excavation Garrod)

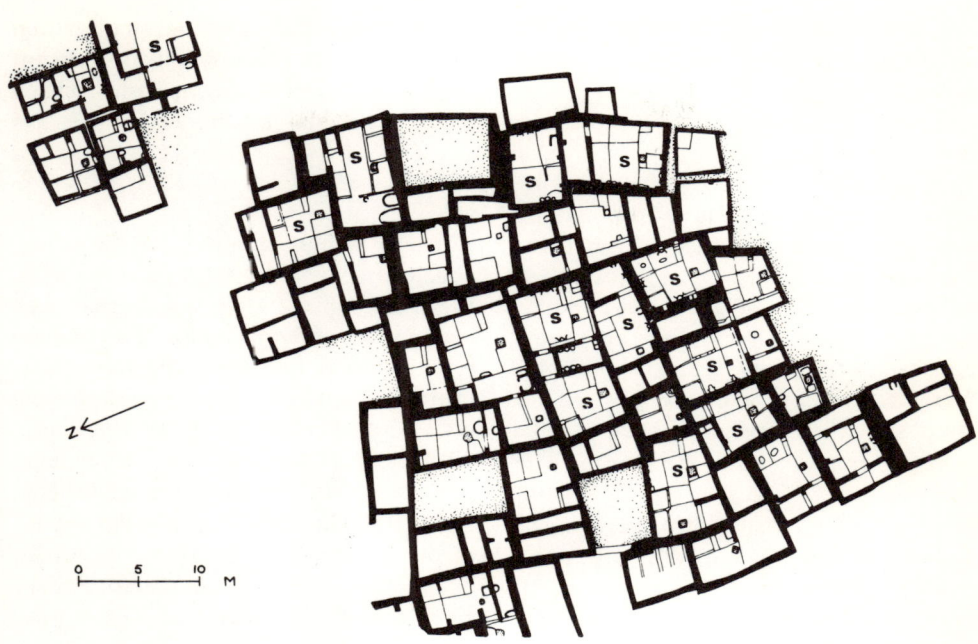

Rectangular houses in the city of Catal Hüyük, Turkey, ca. 10,000 years ago. (Excavation Melaart)

Our knowledge of Jericho is more restricted because only a small area of the site has been excavated. The ancient city is situated near the Dead Sea, whose properties may have played the same role as the obsidian quarries of Çatal. Jericho could have been a centre for extracting and trading salt and asphalt; the latter could have been used to glue flint tools into handles and also as the fluid-proof lining of containers. No great religious centre was unearthed at Jericho but a massive city-wall, built of stone, and a tower eight metres high were uncovered which testify to the importance of the site. Çatal Hüyuk, on the other hand, was not surrounded by a wall; the city had another means of defence — doorless houses adjoining each other so as to form a closed quarter. (Entrance to the rooms was through openings in the roofs, to which removable ladders seem to have provided the only access.)

When, later on, the numerous city-states of Mesopotamia and Egypt emerged during the fifth millenium, all were fortified. They clearly functioned as economic, religious and administrative centres. Writing now appears, and the written documents as well as the archaeological record show a type of social organization and a division of labour, essentially similar to our own. Part of the citizens were not food producers but full-time governors, administrators, priests, merchants, architects and technicians of various types who worked on public constructions which were sometimes gigantic, such as city walls, temples and granaries. The maintenance of order, warfare, and land and sea transportation demanded specialized personnel as well.

The phenomenon of urbanization, then, has a threefold characteristic: the city functions as a cultural and administrative centre for surrounding settlements; division of labour into a variety of occupations apart from food production; and the rise of a class of intellectuals who, by means of the written word, maintain inter- and intra-group cultural relations. At the same time, part of the population — probably the majority — remain food producers. Thus, while an early city was capable of fulfilling any one of the functions of a village, no village is able to fullfil any of the functions of a city. This definition holds true from the beginning of urbanization up to the onset of the Industrial Revolution, when cities became further specialized as technological centres completely dependent on rural settlements for their food supply.

4. *Material Culture*

The beginning of urbanization which, in the Near East, coincided with the onset of the Holocene period was marked by several changes in the material culture, for which the term Neolithic is applied. The round-shaped houses of the final stage of the Palaeolithic were replaced by rectangular structures, both in the cities of Jericho and Çatal Hüyuk and in smaller settlements. In Jericho, sun-dried mud bricks made their first appearance. Floors were commonly plastered and sometimes painted. (Plaster and hardened clay were occasionally used even earlier. For example, a female figurine about 25,000 years old found in Czechoslovakia was made of baked clay mingled with ashes and bone fragments.)

In the Neolithic tool-kit new elements appeared side by side with old ones. Thus mortars and sickle blades were of more varied types than before. For the first time, stone arrow-heads* of extremely diverse types became a characteristic element in the tool-kit. Stone axes*, adzes* and chisels* made their first appearance, and in substantial quantities. If the interpretation that

Various forms of arrowheads from the early Neolithic period, 10,000–8,000 years ago

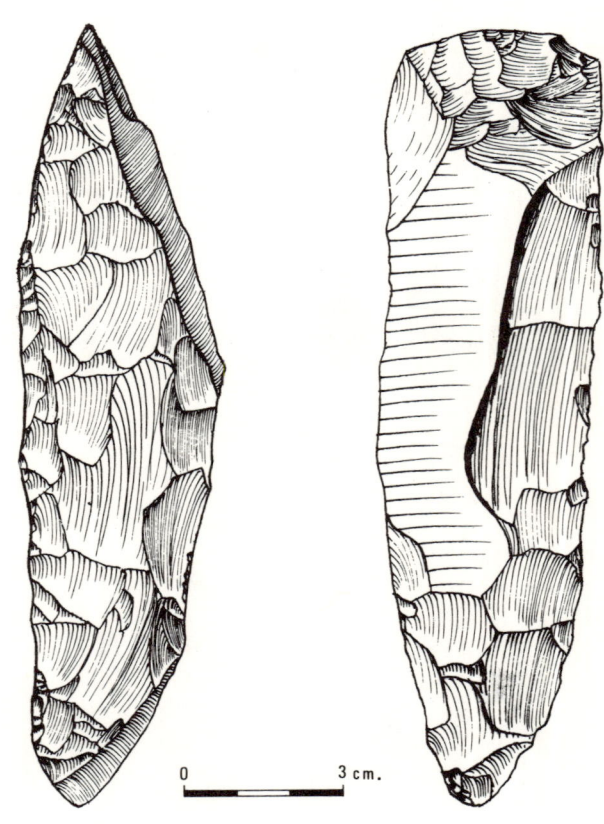

0 ⊢————⊣ 3 cm.

Adze

they were used for wood-working is correct, then we may infer that lands suitable for farming were used up and consequently the clearing of virgin forests and felling of trees became necessary.

The great variety in the types of tools — especially of arrow-heads — denotes a growing rate of temporal and spatial differentiation. The sedentary way of life gave rise to cultural areas of a more restricted size than ever before — sometimes these occupied a single valley or even a village.

Japan is outstanding in the world because of its production of pottery as far back as 14,000 years ago. Elsewhere, the most ancient pottery appeared between 9000 and 7000 years ago, depending on the region. We have already noted that the properties of clay were known prior to that time. Apparently, the necessity for pottery vessels was not previously felt. The need to manufacture pottery might have arisen when containers of animal skins became harder to obtain; in other words, when the cost of a suitable skin rendered the manufacture of pottery more economical and worth while.

The Mesopotamian and Egyptian city-states possessed that element of

Pictographic business document on a stone tablet, Mesopotamia, ca. 5,500 years old. Circles stand for numbers

material culture which ends prehistory: writing. The oldest deciphered written documents deal with public and private possessions such as land, seeds, animals and slaves. Writing began to be regularly practised — the word *invention* is deliberately avoided here — when population pressure on arable land had apparently reached a crucial threshold. According to one estimate, population density in ancient Sumer was comparable to that of modern Egypt. Under these circumstances, co-ordination of daily activities became so complex that memorizing no longer sufficed.

IN RETROSPECT

Recent research has greatly modified our view of the process of humanization. Of particular relevance are the nature and the duration of the process.

The continuity between man and animal now appears to be not only anatomical, as hitherto accepted — the socio-cultural aspect is to be considered as well. Among animals, the presence of a certain learned behaviour (that is, culture) implies that in the human past there must have existed a period of "in between", which we have termed 'The Initial Human Phase'. Humanization increases through the fire-maker of the Intermediate Phase to the Man who, becoming aware of time and death, reached the level of humanity to which we all belong.

What appears to be a fundamental trait throughout the process of humanization is a growing disharmony between man and nature. Disharmony did not originate with modern technology as one might be inclined to feel; modern technology simply brought about its culmination. If harmony means a smoothly functioning system, with no one constituent disturbing any other, then any action upon the system, any change in the environment (in man's case) evidently implies that there was a disturbance somewhere. From this point of view there is no basic difference between man's changing the environment of a cave by fire or that of the moon by more sophisticated means. Both acts disclose disharmony with nature. Disharmony is equally disclosed by man's simple, basic question, "Why?" "Why" could be asked only when nature had ceased to constitute a clear and self-evident entity; in other words, when man had cease'd to be an integral part of that entity, of the system. A system can only be observed and questioned by an 'outsider'.

Man disharmonizes with nature through both the material and spiritual parts of his culture. The role of the material culture, or technology, is evident. But the role of the spiritual part of culture — philosophy and religion — is even more decisive, since through it man accords himself the right to alter and exploit nature, and determines the extent to which this right applies. While all men have accorded themselves the right to exploit and modify nature and all do so, cultures differ markedly in the extent of their self-permission. A most permissive philosophy in this respect appears in the divine blessing in Genesis, i, 26-90.

"And God said, Let us make men in our image after our likeness: and let them have dominion over the fowl of the air, and over the cattle, and over all the earth, and over every creeping thing that creepeth upon the earth . . . And God blessed them, and God said unto them, Be fruitful, and multiply, and replenish the earth, and subdue it: and have dominion over the fish of the sea, and over the fowl of the air, and over every living thing that moveth upon the earth."

The right to exploit is thus accorded and commanded in the same time. The words used are "dominion" and "subdue". Along with specified items, "all the earth" is permitted for exploitation. There is no hint for limitation or refraining from abusive, destructive exploitation. Other cultures view man in a less dominant position in nature, with a more limited right of exploitation (some American Indians, for example).

The extremely long duration of the process of humanization is another discovery of modern research. The oldest human culture presently known is dated to some three million years ago, and a still older date seems only a matter of further research. Even this known date (three times older than was believed just twenty years ago) shows how misleading is the belief that civilization began in ancient Sumer or Egypt, with the first written documents five or six thousand years ago. Seeking to understand the human phenomenon through this tiny portion of human history can be equated to reading only the last paragraph of a book. Indeed, art, religion and science are far older than the first written documents. Furthermore, the study of prehistoric notations now underway may push the beginning of written history much farther back in time than we can now imagine.

In the preface to this book we said that worrying about the future lies behind the study of the past. What can be learned then from the past? Man witnesses a growing alienation between himself and nature, an increasing replacement of the natural environment by a man-made one. We are aware of the ensuing problems of population growth, aggression, shortage of food and energy resources. Knowledge of the past shows that actually we are faced with two different sets of problems: one of which is the fear of death and the anxiety caused by it which, when excessive, causes pathological aggression.[27] The fear of death seems a relatively recent companion of man and, as far as the archaeological and historical record can be judged, man has never yet been able to cope satisfactorily with it. Human culture would not have been what it is without anxiety, but the cultural means man has devised to cope with excessive anxiety are imperfect. This problem is not yet widely understood and constitutes, in my view, the most serious problem with which we are confronted.

The second problem is stress on the environment. However serious, man has dealt with this problem during his entire existence. Food, raw material and population pressure are perfectly well understood by man because of his long struggle with them. And, unlike his inability to deal with the fear of death, man has many times shown his admirable ability to overcome ecological problems. If past and present ecological crises are weighed in their respective technological context then, at present, we are better off than ever before.

APPENDIX ON STONE TOOLS

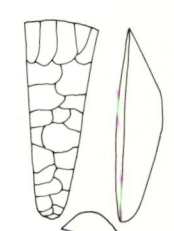

ADZE Implement with the contour of a modern axe; retouched all over and always asymmetrical in cross-section: one face flat and the other raised. The section may be trapezoidal, triangular of semi-circular.

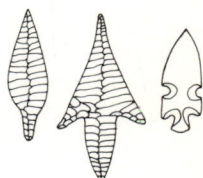

ARROWHEAD Pointed implement, for hafting at the tip of an arrow shaft. Various purposes and hafting techniques have led to a rich diversity of forms; the main classes are tanged, barbed and notched.

AWL Elongated, narrow point, retouched on both sides.

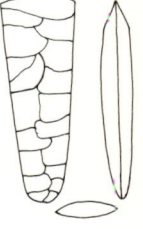

AXE Implement shaped much like the modern tool; retouched on both faces and symmetrical in cross-section, in contrast to the adze.

BURIN or GRAVER Implement with a narrow, somewhat pointed working edge made by removal of a long, narrow spall from the edge of the flake.

CHISEL Narrow, elongated implement with parallel edges, re-touched all over; triangular or quadrangular in cross-section.

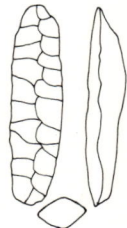

CHOPPING-TOOL Implement having a more or less sharp edge made by flaking one edge of a stone, the surface otherwise remaining unmodified. Crude in appearance, this is considered the earliest man-made tool.

CLEAVER Related to the handaxe family and, like it, is re-touched on both faces; distinguished by its axe-like working edge, whereas most handaxes are pointed or rounded.

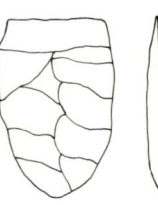

DENTICULATE Having a series of teeth, in the form of a saw, retouched along the edge of a flake.

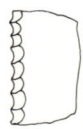

END-SCRAPER or **GRATTOIR** Flake or blade with its short edge retouched to a more or less circular shape. In scientific literature, the French term *grattoir* is often used to avoid confusion with the implement called "scraper".

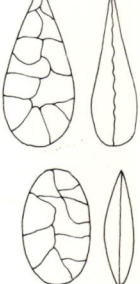

HANDAXE Implement retouched all over into a variety of forms, with two major classes: pointed and rounded.

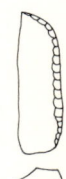

KNIFE Flake with one edge blunted for holding, the opposite edge being left sharp for cutting.

LEVALLOIS TECHNIQUE Elaborate technique of flaking, where the knapper predetermines the shape and size of his product by a series of preparatory flakes (themselves waste products) which create a desired pattern of ridges on the core; a final blow is then given to separate a flake of the desired shape from the core. Flakes and points alike can be produced by this technique, each requiring its own suitable preparation.

MICROLITH Tiny stone implement, between 5 and 50 mm long but not exceeding 12 mm in width, for hafting in bone or wood to form composite tools. Extremely variable in shape, there are two major groups: geometric — rectangular, triangular or lunate; and non-geometric.

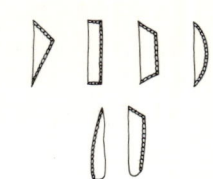

NOTCHED Having a concavity retouched to form a working edge.

SCRAPER Flake with long edge retouched to form a straight, convex or concave working edge; if the short edge is worked, it is called an "end-scraper".

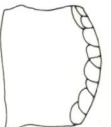

SICKLE-BLADE Implement with three retouched edges and a fourth edge left sharp for cutting; the latter edge is occasionally denticulated. Several such blades were set in a row in wooden or bone handles, and were used in the reaping of cereals, much in the manner of a modern sickle.

SPHEROID Implement rounded by removal of flakes over its entire surface, and varying from the size of a fist to that of a head.

ILLUSTRATION SOURCES

Avraham Ronen, P. 12–13. Drawings by Avraham Ronen, P. 28–33, 41–43, 45, 56, 60–63, 67, 70, 84, 89–90. After Thurville Petre, P. 14. De Sonneville-Bordes, P. 15. Gaussin and Bordes, P. 16. Mission Archéologique Française en Israel, P. 16–17. Irven de Vore, P. 20. After Van Der Kloet, P. 22. Massada, P. 37–40, 73–76. Bordes, P. 52. Vandermeerch, P. 54. Prehistorische Sammlungen Ulm, P. 58. A. Marshach, P. 58. Brno Museum, P. 59. Bosihski, P. 59. Drawings by Ofra Kamar, P. 67, 72. Department of Antiquities and Museums, State of Israel, P. 59 (Photo by David Harris). Perrot, P. 78. Melaart, P. 81. Friedman and Burian, P. 83, fly-leaf.

SOURCES

1   Maslow, A.H., 1963. The Need to Know and the Fear of Knowing. *J. General Psych.* 68:111–25.
2   Clark, G., 1966. Prehistory and Human Behavior. *Proc. Am. Phil. Soc.,* 110:91–99.
3   Piveteau, J., 1973. *Origine et destinée de l'homme.,* Mason, p.v.
4   Spaulding, A.C., 1968. Explanation in Archaeology, in Binford, S.R. and L.R. (eds.), *New Perspectives in Archaeology,* Aldine, pp. 33–40.
5   White, L.A., 1959. *The Evolution of Culture,* McGraw-Hill, p. 8.
6   Deetz, J., 1967. *Invitation to Archaeology,* Natural History Press, p. 45.
7   Goodenough, W.H., 1971. *Culture, Language and Society,* Addison-Wesley Pub. Co., p.19.
8   Mann, A., 1972. Hominid and Cultural Origins. *Man* (N.S.), 7:372-386.
9   Teleki, G., 1972. The Omnivorous Chimpanzee. *Sci. Am.* 226:33-42.
10 Levi-Strauss, C., 1963. *Structural Anthropology,* Penguin, p. 46.
11 Pfieffer, J.E., 1969. *The Emergence of Man,* Harper and Row, p. 283.
12 Pilbeam, D.R., 1968. The Earliest Hominids, *Nature* 219:1335–38.
13 Isaac, G.Ll., R.E.F. Leakey, A.K. Behrensmeyer, 1971. Archaeological Traces of Early Hominid Activities East of Lake Rudolf, Kenya. *Science,* 173:1129–34.
14 Bordes, F., 1971. Allocution, in *Origine de l'homme moderne,* UNESCO, p. 295-6.
15 Howell, F.C., 1966. *Early Man.* Life Nature Library, pp. 85–100.
16 Margalef, R., 1968. *Perspectives in Ecological Theory,* Univ. of Chicago, p. 97.
17 Bordes, F., 1972. *A Tale of Two Caves,* Harper and Row, p. 62.
18 Solecki, R.S., 1971. *Shanidar, the First Flower People,* Knopf.
19 Marshack, A., 1972. *The Roots of Civilization,* McGraw-Hill.
20 Martin, P.S. and H.E. Wright, Jr., (eds.), 1967. *Pleistocene Extinctions,* Yale Univ. Press.
21 Stekelis, M. and O. Bar-Yosef, 1965. Un habitat du Paléolithique Supérieur à Ein-Gev (Israel). *L'Anthropologiee* 69.176–83.
22 Hole, F., K.V. Flannery, J.A. Neely, 1969. *Prehistory and Human Ecology of the Deh Luran Plain.* Univ. of Michigan, Memoire 1.
23 Lee, R.B., 1968. *In* DeVore, I. and R.B. Lee (eds.), *Man the Hunter.* Aldine, pp. 30–48.
24 Kenyon, K.M., 1957. *Digging up Jericho.* Ernest Benn.
25 Mellaart, J., 1966. *Earliest Civilizations of the Near East.* McGraw-Hill, pp.81–101.
26 Longacre, W.A., 1970. *Archaeology as Anthropology: A Case Study.* Univ. of Arizona Anthropological Papers 17.
27 Kubler-Ross, E., 1969. *On Death and Dying.* Tavistock, p. 12–13.

INDEX